Frederic Kidder

History of the First New Hampshire Regiment in the War of the Revolution

Frederic Kidder

History of the First New Hampshire Regiment in the War of the Revolution

ISBN/EAN: 9783337115715

Printed in Europe, USA, Canada, Australia, Japan

Cover: Foto ©ninafisch / pixelio.de

More available books at **www.hansebooks.com**

HISTORY

OF THE

First New Hampshire Regiment

IN THE

WAR OF THE REVOLUTION.

BY

FREDERIC KIDDER.

ALBANY:
JOEL MUNSELL.
1868.

PREFACE.

THE story of the American Revolution has been often written, and most readers are familiar with its prominent features of toils, privation and battles, as well as with the lives of its noted warriors and statesmen. But history like science and the arts is progressive, and we now desire to see details, we wish to know more of the every day life of that period, the names and doings of the humbler officers and men who were the participators in the long marches and sufferings, and also in the battles which produced such glorious results. But so far our history seems deficient in these particulars, as well as in giving us any information of the manner in which regiments were raised, armed, clothed, and supplied with the resources for war. We now find in some of the histories of regiments in the late rebellion details that will supply the want of future readers and historians, but I think no history of a revolutionary regiment has ever yet been published, and it would appear to be difficult now to find materials for such a purpose. Having ventured to attempt it, it may be proper to give some account of the way these materials were procured and the reason for now making them public, as well as the motives which prompted it. A few years ago I met with the journal of an officer in a New Hampshire regiment in the Revolution, and obtained a copy. About a year ago in a search which I made for another purpose in the State House at Concord, I saw what proved to be the pay master's ledger, containing the names, rank and other particulars of every man who served in the First New Hampshire regiment from Jan. 1, 1777 to Jan. 1, 1782. Having obtained the loan of the volume I commenced preparing the material for printing, but soon found I was deficient in the rolls for the succeeding years as well as many other necessary papers. About this time I learned that the paymaster's papers were in the hands of his son James Blake Esqr., of Dorchester. On visiting him he freely tendered me the use of a large quantity of documents referring to this regiment, many of which aided me in this work, and from all these and a few brief extracts from printed volumes this book has been compiled.

It would have been easy to have much enlarged this volume by giving particular accounts of the battles in which the regiment participated, or by extended notices of its four celebrated commanders, Stark, Cilley, Scammell, and Dearborn, whose names are bright in the annals of New Hampshire and add lustre to the history of the nation. But I desired to avoid to any extent reprinting any thing that already could be found in our histories, but rather to give the minute details that these manuscripts furnished of the way in which companies were raised, regiments formed, and the statistics showing the relative rank, pay and rations, as also the laws, rules and materials for clothing of these troops.

The history of a regiment — whose organization is coeval with the commencement of the Revolutionary war, and whose term of service extended beyond its close — who fought bravely at Bunker

Hill, Trenton, Saratoga, Monmouth, Yorktown, and other fields, will I hope contain facts that will commend it to lovers of American history, now and in the future.

In conclusion I would say, that my only motive in preparing this work has been to preserve the names and record the services of the men who aided in achieving our independence, and to contribute some enduring memorial towards the history of my native state.

BOSTON, *July*, 1868.

CONTENTS.

	PAGE.
INTRODUCTORY,	1
ROLL OF OFFICERS,	9
REORGANIZATION,	11
FORM OF ENLISTMENT,	14
LIEUT. THOMAS BLAKE'S JOURNAL,	25
RETURN OF KILLED, WOUNDED AND MISSING IN THE ACTION OF SEPTEMBER 19, 1777,	35
CLOTHING REGULATIONS FOR THE ARMY,	57
DEPRECIATION OF CURRENCY,	80
ROLL OF THE REGIMENT 1780 AND 1782,	81, 85
LIST OF OFFICERS UNDER COL. CILLEY, 1780,	82
LIST OF OFFICERS 1776 AND 1781,	84
ALLOWANCE TO OFFICERS,	86
BIOGRAPHICAL SKETCHES OF OFFICERS,	90
ENLISTED MEN WHO SERVED IN THE REGIMENT, 1777 TO 1782,	131
ROLL OF MEN, NON-COMMISSIONED OFFICERS AND SOLDIERS, 1782,	162

THE HISTORY

OF THE

FIRST NEW HAMPSHIRE REGIMENT.

WHEN the news of the opening of the revolution by the attack of the British forces at Lexington, and their repulse at Concord, on the 19th of April, 1775, went through the country with a speed never before known, the men of New Hampshire were at once on their way to Cambridge, where, seeing that the war was commenced, the leaders, most of whom had seen service in the French wars, felt the necessity of an immediate organization. On the 21st of April, a convention of delegates from many of the towns in the province met at Exeter, when it was "voted that Col. Nathaniel Folsom be desired to take the chief command of the troops who have or may go from this government to assist our suffering brethren in the province of Massachusetts Bay, and to order for the troops the necessary supplies, etc." Subsequently the convention transmitted a letter to the government of Massachusetts, in which they say: "But this body, though heartily willing to contribute in every advisable method to your aid for the common safety, judge it not expedient now to determine upon the establishment of an army of observation, as the towns in this government are not generally represented." "But it is recommended in the meantime to the towns in this colony to supply the men gone from it with provisions and the other necessaries, and from the spirit of the people you may expect their aid, should the emergency require it."

In the meantime, the committee of safety for Massachusetts took the initiative in organizing the large number of troops which had assembled at Cambridge, and on the 26th of April, they issued a commission as colonel to John Stark with "beating orders," and under this he enlisted eight hundred men "from the tap of the drum." Capt. James Reed from Cheshire county, and Paul Dudley Sargent from Hillsborough county, also received commissions as colonels, which were given and accepted with the condition to continue "till New Hampshire should act." Col. Stark having a high reputation as an officer, soon raised fourteen companies, while Reed and Sargent only enlisted four companies each for some weeks.

Upon the convention at Exeter deciding to organize a military force and adopt the regiments then at Cambridge as a part of it, Col. Reed visited that body, and was commissioned as colonel of one of these regiments. But Stark finding himself in command of the largest regiment in the army, and jealous that Gen. Folsom should have been made a brigadier, and so outrank him, would not come into the arrangement. And when Gen. Folsom ordered him to make a report of his regiment, Stark paid no attention to his order. On the 30th of May, Stark received orders from the convention to report to that body in person. Upon this he went to Exeter, and matters were now arranged to his satisfaction. His regiment was called the First New Hampshire regiment, and was to consist of *twelve* companies, while the other regiments were to contain ten companies each: under this arrangement he received a commission as colonel.

The New Hampshire troops were quartered at Medford, from whence Stark and Reed's regiments marched on the 17th of June to take part in the battle on Bunker hill: the record of that day, and the part taken in it by these regiments, forms a portion of the history of the country. During the summer and autumn, these regiments were stationed at Winter hill, where fortifications had been raised.

After the evacuation of Boston, in March, 1776, Stark was ordered with his regiment to New York, and during the summer they went with the expedition to Canada, and on the return of that army they proceeded to Philadelphia, where they were under the command of Washington, and formed a part of Gen. Sullivan's brigade.

While they were slowly retreating through New Jersey, the term for which these regiments had enlisted expired. The army, on which the hopes of the country now rested, had dwindled to a remnant of what it had been. It was poorly clad, fed and paid. They were opposed by a well appointed British force of more than double their number, thoroughly disciplined and completely furnished with every needed supply.

In this discouraging condition, Washington made an appeal to these regiments to remain with him till the season for active service was over, and the enemy had retired to winter quarters. To this appeal an assent was made, and the result of that decision will now be given. Not intending to enlarge on the exploits of this period, which have so often been carefully written, we have passed lightly over the battle of Bunker hill, as well as the march to New York, and the part this regiment took in the expedition to Canada, and the retreat. But the events of December, 1776, and the brilliant action in which the First New Hampshire regiment took so prominent a part would seem to require some more definite details. The following is mainly taken from Judge Potter's *History of Manchester, N. H.*

The affairs of the Americans were now in a desperate condition. Washington's army (which now included the New Hampshire troops), poorly paid, and as poorly clad, had been forced to retreat through New Jersey, before the powerful forces of Cornwallis and Howe, and that state was in the power of the enemy. An insurrection in favor of the royal cause was feared in Philadelphia. And to add to Washington's perplexities under all these difficulties, the time of enlistment of the New England troops, on which he most relied, had expired. All these circumstances were known to the enemy, and Gen. Washington feared they would cross the Delaware and take Philadelphia.

In this posture of affairs, Washington determined on offensive measures, and, if possible, to strike a blow, that while it would surprise and intimidate the enemy, should inspire confidence in the people for their army and the cause. The British forces were distributed through the most important towns in New Jersey, four thousand men being posted on the Delaware at Trenton, and in that neighborhood. These were under the command of Col. Ralle, a Hessian officer of distinction. Count Donop, another Hessian officer of merit, was at Bordentown, lower down on the Delaware, with a brigade of Hessians, and there was another force as low down as Burlington. Deeming the affairs of the Americans in a state of desperation, the British commanders were unwary, and lax in discipline.

This was favorable for Washington. He determined to cross the Delaware and attack the British in their fancied security. In order to better accomplish this, he divided his force into three divisions. Gen. Irvine with the Pennsylvania regulars and New Jersey militia, were to cross at Trenton and secure a bridge below that town, and thus cut off their retreat in that direction. Gen. Cadwallader with the Pennsylvania militia, was to cross at Bristol, and attack the force at Burlington, while the main force under Washington, consisting mainly of troops from New England, was to cross at a ferry nine miles above Trenton and attack Ralle's forces then in possession of that town.

The attack was planned for Christmas night, December 25, 1776, when it would be likely that the enemy were celebrating that festival.

The division under Irvine failed. It was extremely cold, and they could not succeed in crossing the river. Gen. Cadwallader succeeded in getting over a part of his infantry, but they returned. Thus, then, two divisions had completely failed; but Washington's division was composed of a different kind of men.

Neither rain, snow, or ice could stop the New England troops. They were delayed some hours, and did not all get across the river till three o'clock in the morning; and it was fully an hour later before they could take up the line of march. The force was divided, Gen. Washington taking the Pennington road, while Gen. Sullivan, with his brigade of New Hampshire troops, marched down a road nearer the river. The orders were to commence the attack as soon as either party reached the town. Col. Stark led the right wing, and, as Wilkinson writes, "dealt death wherever he found resistance, and broke down all opposition before him." When Stark's troops reached Trenton, about eight o'clock in the morning, a company under the command of Capt. Eben Frye of Pembroke, a veteran who served more than eight years in this regiment, was among the first to alarm the astonished Hessians by driving in their outpost.

As they took refuge in a house, Col. Stark directed Capt. Frye to dislodge them. One of his sergeants with a squad of men and a piece of timber broke in the door, and, using their bayonets freely, soon silenced the party. Col. Ralle attempted to form his astonished troops, but was soon mortally wounded, and his troops retreated towards Princeton, when Washington, discovering their intent, ordered a party by a cross road to cut them off. Capt. Frye's company was the foremost in the movement, and so earnest were his soldiers in the pursuit, that they produced disorder in the ranks, some of them being far ahead. Capt. Frye being very corpulent was soon tired out and could not keep up, and as they were so desirous of pressing on he told them they might follow Sergt. Stevens, which they did. Stevens soon led them into a piece of woods, and lay in waiting for the Hessians to pass. Soon a company of them came up on the run, and, as they came opposite our party, they rushed out upon them uttering a terrific yell. The astonished Hessians threw down their arms and surrendered. Stevens and his men soon had their guns secured, and when the Hessians found they had surrendered to only sixteen men in tattered dress and some bare footed, they attempted to recover their arms; but seeing other Americans coming up they desisted, and Stevens and his squad of sixteen marched his sixty prisoners into Trenton in triumph. As the retreat of the main body was cut off, most of them surrendered, only about five or six hundred escaping. The number that surrendered as prisoners was twenty-three officers and eight hundred and eighty-six men; the killed and wounded amounted to between thirty and forty; while the Americans lost but two killed and six wounded. Washington recrossed the Delaware with his prisoners that night. The effect of this battle was most wonderful: it infused new life into the patriots and their cause.

On the 28th of December, only two days later, Washington again crossed the Delaware, and took possession of Trenton.

The British held Princeton with a considerable force, and soon advanced towards Trenton, determined to try a battle in the open field, and some skirmishing was done, ending with a brisk cannonade, between the belligerent armies, which closed with daylight. Soon after this, Washington ordered his camp fires lighted, and leaving a small guard to carry out the deception, silently withdrew his baggage, followed by his whole force, and took a circuitous route to Princeton. Three regiments of British soldiers had been left at Princeton, and to attack these was the object of our general. He came near surprising them all, but a regiment happening to be on the way to Trenton, they met, and a battle ensued. Gen. Mercer led the advance, mainly consisting of Pennsylvania militia, which soon gave way, and Gen. Mercer was killed in an attempt to rally them. They continued to retreat, and were soon in disorder.

At this moment, Gen. Washington came up with the New England troops, who fought with such spirit, that the enemy soon gave way and retreated into Princeton, our troops closely following them. Here a sharp engagement took place, in which about one hundred of the British were killed, and over three hundred taken prisoners; the rest escaped.

In the morning the British army who had waited, watching Washington's decoy fires, were surprised to find an empty camp; and the army they had expected to attack, were nowhere to be seen. Soon the sound of the cannon near Princeton was heard, and fearing they should be attacked, they retired to Brunswick. In both of those battles, the New England troops did most of the fighting, and no regiment was more conspicuous than that commanded by Col. Stark, which contained many of the men that composed the regiment, whose future movements it is our duty to detail. The following is the roll of officers in 1775 and 1776:

ROLL OF THE OFFICERS OF THE FIRST NEW HAMPSHIRE REGIMENT.

John Stark, Colonel.
Isaac Wyman, Lieutenant Colonel.
John Moore, Major.
Andrew McClary, Major.
Abiel Chandler, Adjutant.
John Caldwell, Quarter Master.
Henry Parkinson, Quarter Master.
David Osgood, Chaplain.

Samuel McClintock, Chaplain.
Obadiah Williams, Surgeon.
Calvin Frink, Surgeon's Mate.
Josiah Chase, Surgeon's Mate.

Companies.

1. Isaac Baldwin, Captain.
   John Hale, First Lieutenant.
   Stephen Hoyt, Second Lieutenant.
2. Elisha Woodbury, Captain.
   Thomas Hardy, First Lieutenant.
   Jonathan Corliss, Second Lieutenant.
3. Samuel Richards, Captain.
   Moses Little, First Lieutenant.
   Jesse Carr, Second Lieutenant.
4. John Moore, Captain.
   Thomas McLaughlin, First Lieutenant.
   Nathan Boyd, Second Lieutenant.
5. Joshua Abbott, Captain.
   Samuel Atkinson, First Lieutenant.
   Abiel Chandler, Second Lieutenant.
6. Gordon Hutchins, Captain.
   Joseph Soper, First Lieutenant.
   Daniel Livermore, Second Lieutenant.
7. Aaron Kinsman, Captain.
   Ebenezer Eastman, First Lieutenant.
   Samuel Dearborn, Second Lieutenant.
8. Henry Dearborn, Captain.
   Amos Morrill, First Lieutenant.
   Michael McClary, Second Lieutenant.
9. Daniel Moore, Captain.
   Ebenezer Frye, First Lieutenant.
   John Moore, Second Lieutenant.
10. George Reid, Captain.
    Abraham Reed, First Lieutenant.
    James Anderson, Second Lieutenant.

The above list corresponds with that printed in Frothingham's *Siege of Boston*, as present at the battle of Bunker hill, and they did not probably vary much for the following year.

THE FIRST NEW HAMPSHIRE REGIMENT AND ITS REORGANIZATION.

We have thus far followed the fortunes and briefly given the record of the First New Hampshire regiment, from its organization at Cambridge, in April, 1775, till its practical dissolution with the close of 1776, and we now commence, under a new arrangement, a continuation of its history. As to whether it was a continuation of the same, or a new organization composed largely from the materials of the old, may be a question. Caleb Stark — who was made adjutant under the new arrangement, January 1, 1777, had been an officer in the former — in writing many years after the war, speaking of Col. Cilley's regiment says: "In this regiment I served in 1775, '6 and '7, devoting all my abilities to form them for action" — thus showing that it was continuous and the same organization; and here we will leave the question for the decision of future historians.[1]

In the fall of 1776, the inconvenience of maintaining an army by annual enlistments and temporary levies,

---

[1] Judge Potter, who is better acquainted with the military history of New Hampshire than any other person, informs me that he considers the first regiment of Col. Stark as the same as that of Col. Cilley.

was severely felt; it had, in fact, nearly brought ruin on the cause; and congress, though slow to act, finally adopted the plan recommended so strongly by Gen. Washington, and passed an act for raising a force by enlisting the men for three years, or during the war. The men were taken for either terms, as they should elect; the officers were to be appointed by congress to serve during the war. New Hampshire was called on for three regiments, and the commanders selected were John Stark, Enoch Poor and Alexander Scammell. This must have been arranged early in November, 1776, for the commissions of those in Stark's regiment bear date November 8th, while many of these officers were serving under him on the Delaware.

In the ledger containing the account of all belonging to this regiment in 1777, kept by the paymaster, the words "engaged November 8, 1776," are placed against the names of all the officers and many of the enlisted men; but their pay did not commence till the first of January, 1777. As but few of the papers which show how men were raised, and regiments organized, are now extant, we propose to insert the documents used for this purpose, which have been preserved by the care of Paymaster Blake, as also the commission of that officer.

Mr. Blake took for his recruiting ground that part of Grafton county bordering on Connecticut river. By his commission it will be seen that it was intended his recruits should form a part of Capt. John House's company, but from some cause House never joined the regiment. He was of Hanover, and had been an officer in 1776. He may have found it impossible to raise the necessary number of men to make up his company, and so some other officer was substituted. He was afterwards a colonel in the militia, and commanded a party of militia from his own and the adjacent towns at the attack by the British and Indians on Royalton.

"To Thomas Blake, Ensign:

You are hereby empowered immediately to enlist a Company to consist of eighty-six able-bodied effective Men, including noncommissioned Officers & Privates as Soldiers in the Service of & for the Defense of the United States, upon the Establishment fixed by the Honorable Congress, with such additional encouragement given by the State of New Hampshire, to continue in that Service till the End of the present War, unless sooner discharged by Congress, & that you cause said Men when so enlisted to pass muster as soon as may be. The noncommissioned Officers to be appointed by the Captain & Subalterns of each Company, & to make due Returns.

 Nov. 11, 1776.   Jon^a Blanchard,
           Steph^n Evans,
           D. Gilman,
           Benjn Giles,

" Committee from the State of New Hampshire."

FORM OF ENLISTMENT.[1]

"We the Subscribers do hereby severally enlist ourselves in the Service of the United States of America, in the Company under the Command of Captain John House, to continue in that Service *three Years from the Date of our Entrance*, unless sooner discharged, and each of us do engage to furnish to and carry with us into the Army a good effective Fire-arm, with a Bayonet fixed thereto, a Cartouch Box, Knapsack and Blanket, and do hereby promise Obedience to the Officers set over us, and to be subject in every Respect to all Rules and Regulations, that are or may be appointed for the ARMY of the aforesaid STATES.

"*Daniel Putnam of Cornish,*
Curtis Cady of Cornish,"
And sixteen others.

It was usual to fix on a certain number of recruits to be raised before a commission could be obtained, and, perhaps it was necessary, that Mr. Blake should furnish the above number to entitle him to have a commission as ensign; but it will be seen that the commission antedated by three days the beating orders, so we may suppose the commission was conditional only. A copy of Mr. Blake's commission in 1776, printed on paper, is inserted: his subsequent ones in 1778, are on parchment, and signed by John Jay.

---

[1] This and the following document were a printed form, and the words in italics were filled in with a pen.

In Congress.

"The Delegates of the UNITED COLONIES of New Hampshire, Massachusetts Bay, Rhode Island, Connecticut, New York, New Jersey, Pennsylvania, the Counties of New Castle and Sussex *on* Delaware, Maryland, Virginia, North Carolina, South Carolina *and* Georgia to *Thomas Blake, Gentleman, Greeting:*

We reposing especial Trust and Confidence in your Patriotism, Valor, Conduct and Fidelity, Do by these Presents constitute and appoint you to be *Ensign of John House's Company, in the First Battalion of New Hampshire Troops, commanded by Col^o John Stark, Esqr* in the Army of the United Colonies, raised for the Defense of American Liberty and for repelling every hostile Invasion thereof. You are therefore carefully and dilligently to discharge the Duty of *Ensign* by doing and performing all Manner of Things thereunto belonging. And we do strictly charge & require all Officers & Soldiers under your Command to be obedient to your Orders as *Ensign*. And you are to observe & follow such Orders and Directions from Time to Time as you shall receive from this or a future Congress of these United Colonies or Committee of Congress for that Purpose appointed or the Commander in chief for the Time being of the Army of the United Colonies, or any other your superior Officer, according to the Rules & Discipline of War in pursuance of the Trust reposed in you. This Commission to continue in Force until revoked by this or a future Congress — *Dated the eighth Day of November Anno Domini* 1776.

" *By Order of Congress*
"JOHN HANCOCK.
" President.

" Attest CHAS. THOMPSON SEC'Y."

" The General Assembly of the State of New Hampshire having appointed the Subscribers a Committee to repair to Ticonderoga to officer & raise two Battalions for the Continental Service & by their Resolve have empowered said Committee to promise & engage the same Encouragement to the noncommissioned Officers & Soldiers in addition to the Encouragement given by the Continental Congress as the State of Massachusetts Bay do give, which is as follows: That each noncommissioned Officer & Soldier who shall enlist into the Continental Service as aforesaid shall be entitled to receive from this State one Blanket annually or eighteen Shillings in Case he shall procure one for himself & procure a Certificate from the Captain of the Company which he belongs, to the Paymaster of the Regiment, provided Congress shall not make Provision for the same. That each noncommissioned Officer & private Soldier who shall enlist into the Continental Service as aforesaid shall be entitled to receive from the Treasury of this State twenty Shillings per Month to be paid him or his Order every six Months during his Continuance in the service in addition to the Pay and encouragement already granted by Congress, provided Congress shall not make any addition to their Wages as established on or before the 19th of September last, and in case the Congress shall not make an increase of Wages less than twenty Shillings per month this State will supply the Deficiency and cause the same to be paid as aforesaid.

" BENJAMIN GILES,
JON$^\text{A}$ BLANCHARD,
STEPH$^\text{S}$ EVANS,
D. GILMAN,
" Committee from N. H."

The following are extracts from the resolves of the Continental congress, viz: "That twenty dollars be given as a Bounty to each noncommissioned officer & private soldier who shall enlist to serve during the present war unless sooner discharged by Congress, that Congress make provision for granting land to the Officers and Soldiers who shall engage in said service and continue therein to the close of the war or until discharged by Congress & the Representatives of such as shall be slain by the Enemy, viz: to each noncommissioned officer & soldier 100 acres. That a suit of clothes be annually given to each noncommissioned officer and private soldier to consist for the present year of two linen hunting shirts two pr. of overhalls a leathern or woolen waistcoat with sleeves, one pr. of breeches a hat or leathern cap, two shirts, two pr. of stockings, and two pr. of shoes, amounting in the whole to twenty dollars or that sum to be paid every soldier who shall procure these articles for himself." There is no date to this paper, but it is supposed that it may be referred to not far from January, 1777. And that the commissioners here named expected to procure soldiers to enlist for the war at Ticonderoga from the regiments whose term of service was expiring there; and that a copy of the above was furnished to any one receiving enlisting orders.

In the committee of safety for N. H., Feb. 25, 1777. The following orders were sent to the Cols. Stark Poor & Scammill, viz:

"Sir: This moment the Committee received by express two Letters from General Washington dated the 7th & 8th of this instant Feb'y wherein he orders all the Troops raised in New Hampshire to march forthwith to Ticonderoga, and directs if the Regiments are not full that they be sent forward by Companies with part of the officers leaving the others to recruit at home and follow after — which command the Committee desire you to carry into execution (as far as relates to your regiment) as fast as possible."

Under this order the enlisting which had been going on all winter was hastened, and every town in the state was visited by some officer, and the selectmen and committee urged to contribute their quota to fill up the companies which would insure the commissions that had been most likely conditionally issued, and so enable the regiment to take the field with full ranks. It is not likely that any actually left the state till the first of March when the roads would be in a better condition for marching and transportation of supplies than a month later. By the following extracts from the records of the committee of safety for the state we know when supplies for these troops were forwarded:

"Exeter, March 4, 1777. Loaded five teams this day for Ticonderoga which makes twenty-four loaded since Friday last."

The men most likely were led on by some officer as fast as they could be collected in companies, or squads, as portions of them would be required to protect the teams after they had passed Number Four, the last stopping place before entering the almost wilderness then existing on the Crown point road to the lake.

The regiment had been recruited and most likely the officers appointed with the expectation that they were to be commanded by Col. Stark; but he was extremely jealous, and as congress had decided to appoint a brigadier from New Hampshire, he thought he was best entitled to it. It was true he had, for near two years, commanded a regiment, had fought with bravery and success, and his claim may have been a proper and valid one, but congress thought proper to give the office to Col. Poor.

Col. Stark took umbrage at this, and repairing to Exeter, communicated the following to the legislature or convention then in session:

"To the Honb'l the Council and House of Representatives for the State of New Hampshire in General Court assembled.

"Ever since hostilities commenced I have as in me lay endeavoured to prevent my Country from being ravaged and enslaved by our cruel and unnatural Enemy, have undergone the hardships and fatigues of two campaigns with cheerfulness and alacrity, ever enjoying the pleasing satisfaction that I was doing my God and my Country the greatest service my abilities would admit of, and it was with the utmost gratitude that I accepted the important command, to which this State appointed me. I should have served with the greatest pleasure more especially at this important crisis, when our Country calls for the utmost exertions of every American, but am extremely grieved that I feel bound in honor to leave the service, Congress having thought fit to promote junior officers over my head, so that I should show myself unworthy the honor conferred on me, and a want of that spirit which should glow in the breast of every officer appointed by this Honorable House in not suitably resenting an indignity, I must (though grieved to leave the service of my Country) beg leave to resign my commission hoping that you will make a choice of some gentleman who may honor the cause and his country to succeed.

"Your most obedient
"And much obliged humble serv't
"JOHN STARK."

The council and house acted upon this March 21, 1777, and passed a vote of thanks, couched in very complimentary language. I cannot obtain the exact date of the resignation, but Lieut. Col. Cilley was promoted to be colonel of the First regiment on the 23d day of February, 1777; and Major Gilman succeeded him in his former place at that date.

The whole regiment did not reach Ticonderoga till late in May, and were located in tents within the old French lines, where they were in expectation of soon seeing the advancing enemy. From this time, a reference to the journal will give the best account of the doings of the regiment, and we shall only give some minute details of battles and particular events that may add to the general facts there stated. From the time of taking the field, the regiment, with those of Cols. Scammell and Dearborn, were formed into a brigade under the command of Brig. Gen. Poor. On the 17th of October, the two belligerent armies were encamped at Saratoga on the banks of the Hudson river. At this time Burgoyne found himself surrounded, and determined to risk all in a general battle, and on this morning drew his army up in a line for combat. The Americans were prompt to enter the contest, and Col. Morgan was ordered to advance into a wooded height, on the enemy's right, while Gen. Poor with his New Hampshire troops, and some others, were ordered to attack the enemy's left, while Morgan's rushed down upon the enemy's right. Poor led his command to the conflict in the most dauntless manner. The New Hampshire line gave their fire; and, with a shout, clearing all interfering obstacles, they charged the British line, with such impetuosity, that it broke and retired from the field, leaving their cannon. The gallant Col. Cilley ordered a detachment of his men to seize and hold one of the pieces, a twelve-pounder. His men obeyed with alacrity, and were preparing under his instructions to turn it upon the enemy. At this moment, the British troops rallied, and forming under the gallant Earl of Balcarras, rushed to the encounter, it being an object of pride to regain their cannon. In this they were partially successful, as at the first onset they forced the Americans to give ground. The twelve-pounder was regained, the gallant soldiers who held it having been killed, wounded or driven back by overwhelming numbers; but their triumph was of short duration; the New Hampshire troops rallied and retook the cannon, driving every resistance before them. Col. Cilley then took charge of the cannon, and, in the excitement of the moment, leaped upon the piece and gave it " a christening." He then with his own hands assisted in loading it and turned it upon the retreating enemy. He did not again leave the piece, for Gen. Wilkinson writes: " Upon visiting the scene of conflict I found the courageous Col. Cilley a straddle on a brass twelve-pounder and exulting in its capture." And here we will mention an exploit of one of the soldiers of the First regiment, recorded in Potter's *History of Manchester* — Thomas Haines, who enlisted from London, but who on his return from the war settled in Concord, where he lived a long life, but finally removed to Loudon, where he died in 1847, aged near ninety years. The record on the paymaster's ledger says: " Wounded at Bemis Heights, and rendered unfit for service, Sept. 19th, 1777."

" He was severely wounded in the encounter for this piece of cannon. He was well known to Col. Cilley and was selected by him among others to man and keep the piece. At the time the British rallied and retook it he was seated astride the muzzle. In this position Haines fought with desperation, killing two soldiers with his gun; one he thrust through the thigh with his bayonet, killing him as quick as if he had pierced his heart. He had attempted to run him through the body, but the British soldier struck the gun down and the bayonet struck him in what is called the pope's eye, and he fell dead. A second soldier came to the assistance of his comrade before Haines had fully recovered his piece, and made a thrust at him with his bayonet, but Haines struck the gun out of his hands with his own, and as the soldier stooped to pick it up,

Haines thrust his bayonet through his head. While in the act of withdrawing the bayonet from the discomfited soldier, Haines was struck in the side of his face with a large musket ball and fell from the cannon to the ground. The ball struck on the right cheek bone, passed through his mouth, carrying away eleven teeth, about a third of his tongue and came out near the left ear. From such a frightful wound he at once became insensible, and lay as one dead on the field for two nights. When the detachment went round to collect and bury the dead, Haines was carried and deposited with the dead to be buried with his comrades. Lieut. Robert B. Wilkins was present, who knew Haines well, and seeing that his body was not stiff insisted that he was still alive. His breast was bare and he was found to have symptoms of life, and he was carried to the hospital and soon recovered so as to be sent to Albany. Here between life and death he lingered for months; at length he recovered so as to rejoin his regiment, and served out his full term of three years, when he returned home."

But our hero could not remain quiet while his services were required in the field, and the record is, " enlisted April 26, 1781, and served to the end of the war."

Let us return to the result of this action, and we find both armies engaged in a furious battle, but the enemy gradually gave way, and when night closed the scene, the Americans had possession of the field, having gained a decisive victory — the enemy having lost in killed, wounded and prisoners over four hundred, and among which were some officers of distinction. The journal gives a minute detail of the killed and wounded on the part of the Americans, and to that interesting account of the doings of the regiment for the next four years we will leave the reader, only making occasional notes to explain some few incidents not particularly mentioned.

LIEUTENANT THOMAS BLAKE'S JOURNAL.

Lebanon, New Hampshire,
May 13, 1777.

I began my march to join Col. Cilley's regiment in the Continental army May 14.

I came to Charlestown No 4[1] where were about one hundred and fifty soldiers belonging to the New Hampshire line going to Ticonderoga.

May 15... We marched from Charlestown for Ticonderoga, and after a very fatigueing march (by reason of the great quantity of rain and the roads being very bad) we arrived at Mount Independence on 21st where we went into barracks.

---

[1] Charlestown No. 4, so named from its being the fourth township as laid out on the east side of Connecticut river, counting from the southwestern corner of the state, was a rendezvous for the assembling of troops from the westerly part of the state in the French and revolutionary wars. The road from there to Lake Champlain which was made for military purposes in the French war, was at that period almost all the way through forests, and for much of the distance over abrupt mountains, and was no doubt very bad.

May 23... The regiment moved over the lake to the old French lines, where we pitched our tents, and Gen. Poor took the command of Ticonderoga and its dependencies.

June 11... Maj. Gen. St. Clair, and B^r Gen. Fermoy are at Ticonderoga, and Gen. St. Clair took command.

June 17... We were alarmed by a party of Indians consisting of about fifty that came up, and lay undiscovered on the road that leads from Ticonderoga to Lake George landing, where they fired upon some men that were passing and killed two, scalping them and took one prisoner. On their return they met a party of our men that had been to Crown point, the Indians fired upon the party but did no damage. The party returned the fire, killed one of the Indians, the rest made their escape.

June 18... Gen. Schuyler who was commanding officer of the northern army, came to Ticonderoga and tarried until the 22d, and then returned to Albany.

June 26... A party of Indians waylaid the road between the mills and lake George, landed, and fired upon two soldiers that were coming from the block house to the landing, killed one, wounded the other and scalped both.

June 28... About 10 o'clock in the evening the garrison were alarmed, the enemy came with some of their gunboats up the lake as far as the Three Mile point, and fired upon our gunboats, but did no damage, and before day they moved back to the Five Mile point.

June 30... The enemy came with their shipping up to the Three Mile point, and landed troops on both sides of the lake, and drew their shipping in a line across the lake; which was 3 ships of 24 guns each, 2 sloops, about 40 gun boats, and about 100 batteaux: at the same time they were landing and pitching their tents; a party (chiefly Indians) came to our lines, fired upon the piquets (that were posted about 100 yards from the works) a few times and then returned.

July 2... About 3 o'clock in the afternoon, a party of the enemy made their appearance on the piece of rising ground (about a mile from the French lines) called Mount Hope, they sent a party to harrass us while they began a battery at that place, it being within good cannon shot. The party first attacked the piquet, who immediately retreated within the lines. They followed them within good musquet shot which they received from the lines, obliging them to retreat. We had 5 men killed and 4 wounded. During the action one prisoner was taken by us, and the same day 2 German soldiers deserted and came into the garrison.

July 3... The garrison was reinforced by about 600 militia from New Hampshire.[1]

July 4... About 200 of the militia came in.

July 5... The enemy got some pieces of cannon up upon the high hill southward of the French lines (called

---

[1] These, it is supposed, were a part of the three New Hampshire regiments, as many of them did not leave home till June.

Mount Defiance) having a battery about finished on Mount Hope, and another on the east side of the lake, opposite the Jersey redoubt.[1]

July 6... About one o'clock in the morning we were ordered out to strike our tents and parade as soon as possible with packs and provisions. As soon as we were paraded we marched over Mount Independence where we found all in a moving posture, the boats and batteaux chiefly loaded, the provisions not all taken in, the clothing chests all broke open, the clothing thrown about and carried off by all that were disposed to take it, and everything in great confusion. About sunrise the last of the boats and the rear guard left the mount, by which time the enemy were in the French lines. The body of the army marched as far as Castleton which is about 30 miles, and the rear guard with the men that could not keep up with the body, tarried at Hubbartown six miles back.[2]

July 7... Early in the morning our rear guard was attacked by about 600 of the enemy; the engagement held some time with considerable loss on both sides; but at length our party not being reinforced re-

---

[1] The abandonment of Ticonderoga was sudden and unexpected. It was caused by the occupation by the British of an high elevation called Edgar hill, which the Americans had deemed impossible to raise cannon; but the enemy soon made a winding road to its summit, and raised a battery which commanded all works occupied by our army. The retreat was hastily made, and much confusion ensued, with an enormous loss of provisions and clothing.

[2] This, I take it, refers to the battle at Hubbardton.

treated;[1] and just as we were ready to march the general had information that the enemy had pursued our boats up to Scheensbury, and had taken all that were sent that way; that the men with the boats were on their way to Fort Ann. The stores and provisions that we lost at Ticonderoga, Mount Independence and Sheensbury were 127 cannon mounted on the batteries, 500 bbls. of powder, and balls answerable, 500 bbls. flour, 1500 bbls. of salt pork, 700 bbls. of salt beef, tents for 4000 men, 5 vessels of from 12 to 16 guns each, all the medicine and chief of the baggage of the army.

July 8... We marched early in the morning, and after a very fatigueing march of five days we came to the North river. In this march we were almost without provisions, entirely without shelter, and the weather chief of the time rainy.

July 13... We marched up the river to Fort Miller, and being informed that the enemy had not left Sheensbury,[2] we tarried there two days to rest.

July 15... We marched up the river 4 miles and encamped on a small hill near the river at Fort Edward.

July 20... Our Indians brought in 2 British prisoners, that they took near Scheensbury.

July 21 ... Seven tories were brought in belonging to the Grants, that had taken up arms against the United States.

---

[1] For a new version of this disastrous retreat, see *Memoirs Gen. Riedesel*, Albany, 1868, 2 vols., 8vo.

[2] Now known as Whitehall, being at the head of Lake Champlain.

July 22... Gen. Arnold came to join the army.

July 24... All the troops left Fort Edward except about 600 who tarried as an advanced guard for the army. This day the Indians killed a captain and a lieutenant, as they were walking in the road between Fort Edward and the army.

July 26... The enemy made an attack upon the outguards at Fort Edward, who retreated into the fort, and the enemy pursued until they received a shot from the fort, and then retreated. The number of the enemy were supposed to be about 2000. After this alarm was over, our party moved down the river to the army, except 100, who still tarried as advance guard.

July 27... In the evening the enemy sent a party in between the army and the fort, but the guard at the fort discovering them, forded the river and came off safe on the other side.

July 28... All the army collected together opposite the island in the river 3 miles above Fort Miller. This day the Indians killed and scalped a woman and her child in a house near Fort Edward.[1]

July 29... The Indians shot one of our centinels as he was walking on his post near the encampment; they likewise came into the road at Fort Miller, and killed and scalped a man and a boy belonging to that place.

---

[1] This was a time of distress and terror. The most terrible accounts of this retreat and the atrocities of the Indians spread through Northern New York and New England. See Stone's *Life of Brant*, 1, 300, *et seq.*

July 31... The army now all lived in huts made of boards that we had collected; as we had no tents since we left Ticonderoga.

We were ordered to take down our huts and raft the boards in the river; in the mean while the waggons were moving the stores down to Fort Miller. After the boards and stores were gone the army marched, but the enemy watching our motion, and seeing us on the retreat, fell on our rear with their Indians, killing and wounding a number. We marched as far as Fort Edward.

Aug. 1... The army waited until the boards and stores were moved by the falls, and the boards rafted again, then moved down the river to Mr. Neals and crossed.

Aug. 2... We were all day getting the boards and scows by Saratoga falls, and rafting again.

Aug. 3... We marched down to Saratoga, leaving only a guard at the ferry of about 60 men commanded by a major.

Aug. 4... Early in the morning as soon as the fog began to blow off, the guard were surprised by the enemy. The first discovery they made, the enemy were coming upon them from every quarter. The guard retreated as fast as possible, toward Saratoga (which is one mile) the enemy pursuing, and took two lieutenants and about 6 or 8 men.

The same morning the Indians came upon one of our piquet guard west of Saratoga, commanded by a lieutenant, fired upon the guard, killing 10 or 12 of them and wounding the lieutenant. The same day the boards were all rafted in large rafts, the stores put upon them, and moved down the river to Stillwater, and in the afternoon the army marched down and encamped.

Aug. 7... The Indians came to the river opposite the encampment, and killed 3 men, took a waggon belonging to the inhabitants of that place. The same day 4 British soldiers deserted and came to our camp.

Aug. 8 & 9... The army lay still, only sending out scouting parties to collect the cattle and move the inhabitants down below the army.

Aug. 10... All the sick, and the hospital stores were moved down to New city.

Aug. 11... Began to move the other stores of the army.

Aug. 12... Gen. Leonard's brigade marched for Fort Stannocks.[2]

Aug. 15... The whole army marched down the river 6 miles and encamped.

Aug. 18... The army moved down to Van Schoyck's island, but Gen. Poor's brigade was posted at Lowdon's ferry, up the Mohawk 3 miles.

Aug. 22... Two regiments of New York troops came and joined Gen. Poor's brigade.

Aug. 23... The two regiments of York troops

---

[1] Perhaps now known as Lansingburgh.
[2] Stanwix?

marched for Fort Stannocks, but after 3 or 4 days march they had information that the enemy had made an attack upon that fort and were defeated, and had returned, for which reason they marched back and joined the brigade.[1]

Aug. 29... A regiment of riflemen commanded by Col. Morgan, came and joined the army.

Sept. 8... The army now having got somewhat recruited and reinforced we began our march up the river again (to meet the enemy) under the command of Gen. Gates, and marched 8 miles.

Sept. 9... We marched as far as Stillwater and encamped.

Sept. 10... We began to fortify on the heights back of Stillwater, and built a floating bridge across the river. The same day the riflemen took and brought into camp three families that were moving to the enemy with all their effects.

Sept. 11... About 7 or 800 of militia came in from Benington.

Sept. 12... The army marched up the river about three miles, and encamped on the high ground about half a mile from the river known by the name of Beman's heights; here we fortified, the enemy then lay at Saratoga.

Sept. 13... Gen. Arnold marched out with his division

---

[1] For a minute account of the operations on the Mohawk, see *Life of Brant*, vol. 1.

and took a view of the enemy's encampment, took 8 prisoners and returned without loss. About 11 o'clock our riflemen fell in with the enemy about 2 miles from our encampment, they being on their march down the river, but after a short engagement were obliged to retreat.

Sept. 19... About 12 o'clock the first N. Hampshire Reg* marched out to meet the enemy. We met them about one mile from our encampment, where the engagement began very closely, and continued about 20 minutes, in which time we lost so many men, and received no reinforcement, that we were obliged to retreat, but before we got to the encampment we met two regiments coming out as a reinforcement, when we returned and renewed the attack which continued very warm until dark, at which time we withdrew and retired to our encampment.

In this engagement the enemy had two field pieces in the field, which we took three or four times, but as it was in the woods, they were not removed.

The number of our men lost to the army in this engagement, is according to the following return :

FIRST NEW HAMPSHIRE REGIMENT.

A Return of the Killed, Wounded and Missing, in the Action of September 19, 1777.

Brigades	Regiments	Killed							Wounded						Missing				
		Lt. Colonels	Captains	Subalterns	Sergeants	Drum and Fif's	Rank and File	Total	Captains	Subalterns	Sergeants	Drum and Fif's	Rank and File	Total	Captains	Lieutenant	Sergeants	Rank and File	Total
General Poor's	Col. Cilley's,																		
	Hale's,																		
	Scammell's,																		
	Courtland's,																		
	Livingston's,																		
	Cook's,																		
	Latimer's,																		
	Total,													164					
General Learned's	Col. Bailey's,																		
	J. Livingston's,																		
	Wiston's,																		
	Jackson's,																		
	Total,							10											9
Rifle Men and Light Infantry	Col. Morgan's,																		
	Majr Dearborn's,																		
	Total,																		
	Whole loss,																		

The loss of the enemy is not known, but supposed to be somewhat larger.

Sept. 24... About 2000 of the militia came in and joined our army. After the action of 19th there were some of the enemy deserted and came into our encampment almost every day. The enemy threw up works at about a mile distant from ours, and nearly in the same direction.

Oct. 7... A detachment of the enemy marched out upon the left of our army, consisting of the grenadiers and light infantry, with 6 field pieces, and posted themselves on a small height in a cleared field about a quarter of a mile from our advanced guard, where they began a cannonade upon the riflemen, and the three Hampshire regiments were ordered out to attack them, which we did, and after a very warm dispute of about half an hour, the enemy were obliged to quit the field and retreat to their works, which they did in great confusion (their horses being chiefly killed) and were obliged to leave their field pieces which fell into our hands, together with about 50 prisoners, and our army followed hard after them, and coming on the lines where the German troops were stationed, forced them and took a number of prisoners, two field pieces and several waggons loaded with ammunition and baggage and by the time we had secured what we had taken at the line it was almost dark, and the troops that had been in action were relieved by fresh troops from our encampment, who tarried at the lines we had taken all night, the British laying about a hundred rods distant.

Oct. 8... The enemy moved their baggage and artillery back from their front lines, and in the night marched their whole army for Saratoga, leaving their sick and wounded in some large hospital tents, with several surgeons to attend them. They burnt most of the buildings as they went, and cut away the bridges; and whenever their waggons or tents or baggage broke down, they knocked the horses on the head and burnt the baggage.

Oct. 9... Our whole army marched in pursuit of the enemy, and came up with them at Saratoga; where we formed a line almost around them on the west side of the river, and a party of militia on the opposite or east side; by which means they could not move without our notice.

Oct. 15... There was a cessation of arms agreed upon between the armies, and proposals for a capitulation, which was agreed upon next day.

Oct. 17... The enemy marched out and piled their arms in front of our army, and marched for Cambridge.[1]

Oct. 18... Our army marched down to Albany.

Oct. 19... Encamped on the high land back of the city.

Oct. 23... Gen. Poor's brigade was ordered to march, crossed the river and encamped about 6 miles below for the night sending our tents down by water.

---

[1] For complete accounts of the battle at Stillwater on Sept. 19th, see *Life of Gen. Stark*, also Lossing. This return of the killed and wounded is most likely as authentic as it could be made.

Oct. 24... We marched to Canterhook, and

Oct. 25... We marched to Claverick.

Oct. 26... Marched to Livingston Mannor the

Oct. 27 & 28... Lay still, being too wet to march.

Oct. 29... We marched about 4 miles, but the rain coming on again obliged us to halt.

Oct. 30... Marched to Rinebeck.

Oct. 31... Marched to Poughkeepsie.

Nov. 1... We took our tents from the boats and dried them.

Nov. 2... We marched to Fishkill and camped. Here we tarried several days, in which time there was a mutiny happened in the brigade, by which one captain and one private lost their lives.

Nov. 12... We marched 10 miles and encamped.

Nov. 13... Marched to King's ferry and crossed.

Nov. 14... We lay still about a mile from the river.

Nov. 15... Marched to New Antrim 18 miles.

Nov. 16.... Marched to Pampton.

Nov. 17... Marched to Morristown.

Nov. 18... Marched to Lormiugten.

Nov. 19... Marched to Amwell.

Nov. 20... We marched to the Delaware, and crossed at Correll's ferry.

Nov. 21... We marched to Warwick.

Nov. 21... Marched to White Marsh, which is about 13 miles from Philadelphia. There we joined the main army under command of Gen. Washington.

Dec. 5... Early this morning we had information

that the greatest part of the British army were leaving Philadelphia to meet us, upon which our tents were all struck, and loaded into the waggons, together with our baggage, and moved off, and the army paraded. In the afternoon they appeared on an eminence called Locust Hill, in front of us, but at the distance of 3 miles, where they tarried all night.

Dec. 6... The enemy marched toward our left, and our army were under arms all day.

Dec. 7... Col. Morgan with the rifle regiment fell in with the enemy, exchanged a few shot and retreated.

Dec. 8... We lay still; and about 2 on morning of

Dec. 9... The rifle regiment and 3 brigades marched out in order to attack the enemy on their own ground at day break; but they moved off for Philadelphia before that time.

Dec. 11... About an hour before day we had orders to prepare for a march from our guard about day break to meet a party of the enemy who were foraging on the other side of the Schuylkill. We marched about 10 miles, and came to the bridge, two brigades crossed, the rest were following, but the enemy met them and taking possession of the heights in front, and on each side of the road leading from the bridge, that our men were obliged to retreat over the river again and there halted, so that neither army could cross. We lay there till almost night; when part of our army marched up the river to Sweed's ford, two miles, to prevent the enemy from crossing at that place.

Dec. 12... About sunset some of our horsemen brought into camp two Hessians they had taken who gave intelligence that there were about 4000 of the enemy over the Schuylkill after forage; and Gen. Sullivan immediately marched in pursuit and crossing the river proceeded as far as the Gulph mills, but having information they had returned to Philadelphia we there halted.

Dec. 16... The army marched to Valley-forge and encamped.

Dec. 23... The ground was staked out for the army to build huts to winter in at this place; which is about 22 miles from Philadelphia. In about a week from this date the army in general moved into their huts, which were built with round logs, and most of them covered with straw and earth; and lay in two lines which extended from the Schuylkill about one and a half miles. In the beginning of February each brigade were ordered to build a breast work in front of their own huts, which was done in a few days. The whole army lay there except two brigades at Wilmington, down the Delaware river, and also about 300 men at Rednar, 7 miles from camp; and 200 at the Gulph Mills about the same distance; each of these two last named parties were relieved every week. There were likewise guards kept about one mile distant from camp, which formed a chain of centinels round the whole encampment, which were relieved daily. The army lay in this posture during the winter

and nothing remarkable happened. [* * *
* *]

May 6, 1778. This day was kept as a day of rejoicing on account of the news of the alliance of France; on which account his excellency Gen. Washington was pleased to release all the prisoners then in confinement, belonging to the Continental army. The whole army was drawn up in two lines, and fired a fu-de-joy, from right to left of the front, and from left to right of the rear lines; which was repeated three times.

June 10... The whole army moved out of their huts, excepting the sick;[1] and pitched their tents in front of the lines. The night after the 17th the enemy left Philadelphia and marched over into the Jerseys.

June 18... At 4 o'clock in the afternoon Gen. Lee's division marched, consisting of Gen. Poor's, Varnum's and Huntington's brigades, three miles over Schuylkill bridge and encamped.

June 19... Marched about 18 miles.

June 20... At 12 o'clock we came to the Delaware river, and crossed at Corell's ferry, marched 3 miles and encamped in Amwell.

June 21... Gen. Lee's division lay still, and Gen. Washington crossed the river and another division of the army.

[1] The regiment suffered severely by sickness during this year.

June 22... The whole army crossed and encamped in Amwell, excepting a party that marched to take possession of the city of Philadelphia.

June 23... The whole army marched down toward the enemy (leaving the tents and baggage), as far as Hopewell township, and halted; but Col. Morgan with his regiment of riflemen and a detachment under his command marched toward the enemy.

June 24... The army lay still, the tents came up and were pitched, a detachment went forward under the command of Gen. Scott.

June 25... Marched to Kingstown, and another detachment went forward under the command of the Marquis De la Fayette.

June 26... Marched to Cranberry town and Gen. Lee went forward with two brigades.

June 27... Marched to Cranberry meadows.

June 28... Marched to Englishtown and there left our packs and coats the weather being very warm, and proceeded as fast as possible in pursuit of the enemy who were then near Monmouth Court House. The forward detachment had attacked the enemy, and Gen. Washington met them on the retreat about one and one-half miles above the Court House. Our artillery set in very briskly, causing a heavy cannonade on both sides, holding for some time until the enemy retreated. Our army pursued about a mile, and then left them. The enemy encamped that night near the Court House; and in the night moved off leaving all their wounded not able to march, numbering about sixty, of whom were five commissioned officers.

June 29... Two brigades marched down to the Court House, as a covering party while they buried the dead. The number of those buried were about three hundred, that of ours sixty. After the dead were buried the whole army marched back to Englishtown.

June 30... Lay still at Englishtown.

July 1... The whole army march to Spotwood, the weather being so excessively hot (the road being for most part through Pitch pine plain) that near one-third of the men were so overcome that they were obliged to stop; many were not able to march until the cool of the evening, and some so overcome they were obliged to be conveyed in waggons.[1]

July 2... Marched to Brunswick.

July 4... This being the anniversary of American independence, it was celebrated in the following manner: The army were drawn up in two lines, with the field pieces attached to brigades, placed in the line of brigades. In the first place there were thirteen cannon fired, then a running fire beginning on the right of the first line to the left and from the left of the rear line to the right; this was repeated three times adding the huzzas!!

July 5... The left wing of the front line marched.

---

[1] This account of the battle of Monmouth, though brief, seems sufficiently complete.

July 6... The right wing marched. We marched 10 miles.

July 7... Marched to Springfield 10 miles.

July 8... Marched to Wardsession 10 miles, where we came up with the other wing of the army.

July 9... We lay still.

July 10... Marched to Storterdam 12 miles and crossed the second river, so called.

July 11... Marched 10 miles to Peramust.

July 12 & 13... Lay still.

July 14... Marched 13 miles to Kirkeat.

July 15... Marched to King's ferry, and Maj. Gen. Baron de Kalb's division crossed.

July 16... Maj. Gen. Baron de Steuben's division crossed.

July 17... Marched to Pickskill (Peekskill) Landing.

July 18... Marched to Croton bridge.

July 19... Lay still.

July 20... Marched to North Castle.

July 24... Marched to White Plains where the whole army encamped (except two brigades which marched for Rhode Island). Here we lay till September, and nothing remarkable happened.

Sept. 11... Three brigades, viz: Gen. Poor's, Learnard's and Patterson's marched. We marched 8 miles.

Sept. 12... Marched 3 miles past Bedford.

Sept. 13, 14, & 15... Lay still.

Sept. 16... Marched to Ridgefield, (Ct.).

Sept. 17... Lay still.

Sept. 18... Marched to Danbury and encamped on the hills east of the town.

Oct. 17... This day being twelve months since Gen. Burgoyne's army laid down their arms, and surrendered themselves prisoners, it was celebrated in the following manner by the troops then at Danbury, under the command of Maj. Gen. Gates. In the forenoon there was a discourse delivered by the Rev. Mr. Evans, chaplain to Gen. Poor's brigade, suitable to the occasion. At one o'clock, there were 13 cannon fired, after which all the officers of the division, the hospital surgeons that were stationed there, and the militia officers of the town, dined together. After dinner the following toasts were drank, and a cannon fired after giving of each: 1. The United States of America. 2. Congress. 3. Gen. Washington and the American army. 4. The American navy. 5. The King of France and our allies in Europe. 6. Count De Estang, and the fleet under his command. 7. Dr. Franklin and the American plenopotentiaries in Europe. 8. Gov. Trumbull and the state of Connecticut. 9. The glorious 24th of December, 1776. 10. The glorious 28th of June, 1778. 11. The glorious memory of Gens. Warren, Montgomery, Mercer, Worster and Nash, with all the virtuous officers and soldiers who have died in defense of freedom and their country. 12. May all citizens be soldiers, and all soldiers be always citizens. 13. The glorious 17th of October, 1777.

Oct. 19... Gen. Poor's brigade moved. We marched 7 miles.

Oct. 20 .. Marched to Woodbury 12 miles.

Oct. 21... Marched to Waterbury 12 miles.

Oct. 22... Marched to Farmington 18 miles.

Oct. 24... Marched to Hartford 12 miles, and encamped on the bank of the river just above the town. Soon after the other two brigades came in and encamped in a line with ours.

Nov. 15... We marched back from the river about 6 miles, and encamped in the woods.

Nov. 20... Gen. Poor's brigade marched to Simsbury, where we took charge of the German troops, that were captured with Gen. Burgoyne, they being on their way to Virginia.

Nov. 21... Marched to New Hartford 12 miles.

Nov. 22... Marched to Norfolk 15 miles, but the traveling was so bad that we were obliged to lay still 2 days for our baggage to come up.

Nov. 25... Marched 3 miles past South Canaan.

Nov. 26... Marched to Kent 15 miles.

Nov. 27... Marched to New Milford 15 miles, where a party of the militia received the German troops.

Nov. 28... Marched to Danbury 15 miles.

Dec. 2... Marched to Redding 5 miles, where we were to build our huts for the winter.

Dec. 4... We began to build our huts, which we finished in a short time, and tarried in them till the 10th of April, and then marched to the high lands on North river, where we went into huts and staid till May 9th 1779, then marched for Easton in Pennsylvania, where we arrived the 18th, and took quarters in the Court House and other spare buildings.

May 19, 1779. Gen. Sullivan arrived at Easton, being appointed to command of the western army.

May 28.... Col. Cilly's regiment marched to Wyoming 12 miles.

May 29... Marched to Pocono point 15 miles.

May 30... Marched to Tuckhannock 10 miles.

May 31... Marched to Locust hill 6 miles, where we came up with Col. Courtland's and Col. Spencer's regiments, who were cutting a road through to Wyoming. We pitched our tents and went to work with them, and a detachment of 200 men from the three regiments marched forward to Wyoming. We worked on the road till June 7, and moved our tents 8 miles.

June 9... Moved 2 miles and encamped.

June 11... Moved 5 miles to Bullock's house.

June 14... Marched to Wyoming 7 miles, and 65 from Easton.

June 17... Col. Cilly's, Courtland's and Spencer's regiments marched up the river to Jacob's Plains 4 miles and encamped.

June 23... Gen. Sullivan came into Wyoming, also 5 other regiments.

July 4... Col. Cilly's and Courtland's regiments crossed the river and marched down two miles toward

Wyoming, and encamped with the rest of Gen Poor's brigade.

July 5... Gen. Poor made an entertainment for the officers of the brigade in commemoration of American independence, and after dinner the following toasts were drank: 1. United States. 2. July 4, 1776, the memorable. 3. The grand council of America. 4. Gen. Washington and the army. 5. The king and queen of France. 6. Gen. Sullivan and the Western expedition. 7. May the councillors of America be wise, and her soldiers invincible. 8. A successful and decisive campaign. 9. Civilization or death to all savages. 10. To the immortal memory of those heroes that have fallen in defense of American liberty. 11. May the husbandman's cottage be blessed with peace, and his fields with plenty. 12. Vigor and virtue to all the sons and daughters of America. 13. May the New World be the last asylum of freedom and the arts.

July 27... Gen. Poor's brigade marched down to Wyoming and encamped with the rest of the army.

July 31... Having all things in readiness, the army began their march up the river. We marched to Lacawaneck 10 miles.

Aug. 1... Marched to Quilutamack 7 miles, and met with so much difficulty in passing some large mountains that ran down to the river, that the rear did not come up till sunrise next morning, for which reason we lay still the second day.

Aug. 3... Marched to Tunkhannick 12 miles.
Aug. 4... Marched to Vanderlip's farm 13 miles.
Aug. 5... Marched to Wylusink 10 miles.
Aug. 6 & 7... Lay still.
Aug. 8... Marched to Standingstone 11 miles.
Aug. 9... Marched to Shesheek 16 miles.
Aug. 10... Lay still.
Aug. 11... Forded the river, and marched to Tioga 5 miles, and there encamped on the point between the Seneca and Tioga branches.
Aug. 12... Toward night we had orders to prepare for a march, and left Tioga just after sunset with one day's provision, leaving all our tents standing, and our baggage in them, with a few men least able to march. Marched all night though very dark and bad traveling; and just at day break next morning reached Chemong, a small Indian town 14 miles from Tioga; but they being alarmed before we could surround the town made off. They had previously moved all their women, children and effects, leaving only about fifty of their warriors as a guard. Gen. Hand's brigade followed them up the river about two miles where they had posted themselves in a very advantageous position. They gave the brigade a shot and ran off. In the meantime we set fire to all the buildings in the town, about twenty, then marched, crossed the river, and destroyed three or four fields of corn, cutting and throwing it in heaps, the corn then being in the milk. While at work on the last field, we were fired upon

across the river by the Indians, killing one and wounding four of our men. The whole of our killed and wounded this day was about 15 or 16. We were not positive of killing more than one of the Indians. In the afternoon we marched back to Tioga.

Aug. 15... A party of Indians came down to the south side of the river, opposite the encampment, and fired upon some men that were tending cattle, killed one and wounding another.

Aug. 16... A detachment of 900 men commanded by Gen. Poor, marched up the river to meet Gen. Clinton's brigade who were to meet us at Tyoga from the Mohawk river.

Aug. 17... The Indians killed one man near the encampment.

Aug. 22... Gen. Clinton's brigade with the detachment sent to meet him came in.

Aug. 26... Three Indians belonging to the Oneida tribe came in to join our army and assist our guides. The same day the army began to march into the Seneca country, leaving a garrison of 500 men; marched 4 miles and encamped.

Aug. 27... Marched 6 miles.

Aug. 28... Thence to Chemong 4 miles.

Aug. 29... We marched about 4 miles, where our advanced guard were fired upon by the enemy from a breast work they had thrown up, of about a quarter of a mile in length, extending from the river to a large range of mountains, which lay parallel with the river. The army halted, and Gen. Poor's brigade marched back of the mountain in order to cross the range in rear of the enemy. In the meantime we kept a few men firing before the breast work in order to arouse the enemy. Gen. Poor's brigade marched round about three miles, and as we attempted to ascend and cross the mountain, were fired upon by the Indians, who gave at the same time a most hideous yell which resounded in the mountains as if covered with them.

The brigade formed line and marched up, receiving a constant fire from them; but as soon as we reached the top they fled, and those at the breastwork at the same time. We had 4 men killed and 32 wounded. There were 11 Indians left dead on the ground.[1] They took off their wounded, as appeared by the blood where they crossed the river. We took two prisoners during the action, a white man and a negro, who informed us there were 600 Indians, 200 Tories and 14 British troops all under the command of Col. Butler. That they had been waiting some time for us, intending to cut off our provisions, and to hinder our further progress into their country.

Aug. 30... We lay still, and in the evening sent the wounded men down to Tioga in boats.

Aug. 31... Marched 10 miles.

---

[1] Sullivan's official account gives minute details of the battle of Newtown.

Sept. 1... Marched to French Katharines 13 miles.

Sept. 2... Lay still.

Sept. 3... Marched 10 miles and encamped on the north side of Seneca lake.

Sept. 4... Passed Appletown and marched 13 miles.

Sept. 5... Marched to Kondar 6 miles.

Sept. 6... Marched 4 miles.

Sept. 7... Marched round the end of Seneca lake to Kanadasaga 13 miles.

Sept. 8... The army lay still; a detachment went up the south side of the lake to destroy a town.

Sept. 9... Marched 8 miles.

Sept. 10... To Kennendaughque 12 miles.

Sept. 11... To Hanneyauyen 13 miles; here we left a garrison of 100 men with part of the flour and ammunition.

Sept. 12... Marched 11 miles.

Sept. 13... After marching 2 miles we came to a town called Keneghses where the army halted to build a bridge over a large sunken place for the troops to cross. In the meantime, part of the riflemen went forward to the next town. On their return within about a mile of the army, they were fired upon by the enemy who had posted themselves on a hill ready to give us a shot as soon as we came out of the swamp. They killed 13 of the riflemen and took two prisoners. Our men being alarmed by the fire, the light troops marched to their relief, on the appearance of which the enemy quit the ground leaving 70 of their packs.

After this we marched to Gaghaheywarahera; the whole of our march to-day being 9 miles.

Sept. 14... We marched two miles and forded the Chinesee river,[1] then 3 miles down the river to a large town called Chinesee Castle, and here found the two men that had been taken the day before cut to pieces in the most barbarous and inhuman manner possible to be conceived. In this town were 180 houses and an exceeding large field of corn, which took the army until the middle of the afternoon next day to destroy, after which we marched about 4 miles.

Sept. 16... We marched to Keneghses.

Sept. 17... Marched to Hannauyan.

Sept. 18... Marched to Kennendaughque.

Sept. 19... Marched to Kanadasaga.

Sept. 20... A detachment of 500 men commanded by Col. Butler were sent off to go up the lake (Keynga on the northeast side; the army marched a little past the end of Seneca lake.

Sept. 21... Another detachment of 200 men under command of Col. Dearborn left us to go up the southwest side of Kenga[2] lake. The army marched 3 miles past Kendai; and

Sept. 24... We met some of our boats 5 miles above Newton, where we halted until the detachments came in; and

---

[1] Probably Genesee.
[2] Cayuga.

Sept. 29 & 30... Marched to Tyoga.

Oct. 4... The army marched for Wyoming, making 14 miles.

Oct. 5... The whole army went on board the boats, except a sufficient number to drive down the horses and cattle, and arrived at Wyoming, on

Oct. 7... About noon.

Oct. 10... Marched for Easton where we arrived

Oct. 15... And encamped near the river.

Oct. 27... Marched toward the North river, and

Oct. 30... Pitched our tents at the mouth of the cove.

Nov. 6... Marched to Plimpton and encamped.

Nov. 24... Marched 15 miles toward the North river.

Nov. 25... Marched to the river and crossed.

Nov. 27... Marched to Crumpond.

Nov. 28... Marched 12 miles.

Nov. 29... Marched to Ridgburry.

Dec. 1... Thence to the place pitched upon for building our huts for the winter, which was about half way between Danbury and Newtown, and next day,

Dec. 2... The ground was staked out and

Dec. 3... Began to build our huts which were finished in about 14 or 15 days. At this place we lay until

April 6, 1780. Thence we marched to West point.

Aug. 4... We left West point and marched to Peekskill and

Aug. 5... Marched to King's ferry but could not cross, as the army were crossing there.

Aug. 6... We crossed the river and marched 4 miles.

Aug. 7... Marched down the river as far as Greenbush.

Aug. 8... Marched to Tappan, Orangetown, where the whole army encamped.

Aug. 23... The army marched down to Jeverich, opposite the upper end of York island.

Sept. 4... The army marched about 6 miles toward Peramus, to a place called Stanrapic.

Sept. 17... Gen. Washington sat off on a journey to Hartford, and left the command of the army to Maj. Gen. Green.

Sept. 20... The army marched up to Tappan and took their old encampment ground.

Sept. 25... Gen. Arnold's plot was discovered, and he made his escape to the enemy; but Maj. Andre, adjutant general to the British army, was taken prisoner. His excellency Gen. Washington was on his return from Hartford, and just arrived at Gen. Arnold's quarters as the plot was first discovered and tarried there a few days, but sent Maj. Andre to the main army.

Oct. 1... A board of general officers sat to examine into the case of Maj. Andre, who reported: *First,* That he came on shore from the Vulture sloop of war, in the night of the 21st of Sept., for a secret interview with Gen. Arnold. *Second,* That he changed his dress within our line, and in a disguised habit passed the works at Stoney and Verplank's points; on the evening of the 22d and on morning of the 23d was taken at Tarry Town, on his way to New York in disguise, and was in possession of several papers, containing intelligence for the enemy. The board do therefore report to his excellency Gen. Washington, that Maj. Andre ought to be considered a spy from the enemy, and agreeable to the laws of nations ought to suffer death. The commander in chief directs the execution of the above sentence in the usual way.

Oct. 2... Maj. John Andre, adjutant general to the British army, was hanged.

Oct. 6... The army marched. Four brigades for West point, under the command of Gen. Green; the rest of the army marched back from the river. Ours with Gen. Green marched to Haverstraw.

Oct. 7 & 8... Marched to West point and the First and Second New Hampshire regiments encamped on Constitution island.

Oct. 25... Crossed the river and marched to Soldiers Fortune, where we began to build our huts for the winter, but did not finish them till the beginning of January, by reason of being so often called down to the lines.

The following acts of congress, relative to the army, are preserved at the end of Blake's journal, and are printed to show the laws and customs at that period:

CLOTHING REGULATIONS FOR THE ARMY.

In Congress, Nov. 25, 1779.

WHEREAS Congress by sundry resolutions, have provided that clothing be furnished to the officers of the line and others, at prices proportioned to their pay, but no enumeration of the articles intended to be comprehended in a suit of clothes having been made, or any rules explicitly laid down for the delivery of or payment for the same.

Resolved, That the following articles be delivered as a suit of clothes, for the current, and every succeeding year of their service, to the officers of the line and staff, entitled by any resolutions of Congress to receive the same, viz: one hat; one body coat; four stocks; four pr. breeches, two for winter, and two for summer; four pr. of shoes; one waistcoat; four shirts; four vests, one for winter, and three for summer; six pr. of stockings, three pr. worsted, and three of thread.

For which articles of clothing the officer shall pay on receipt thereof, one-half more than the prices at which the same were currently sold before the commencement of hostilities in April, 1775.

And for this end the purchasing agents employed on Continental account, shall transmit to the clothier general, with the clothing they shall respectively purchase, the prices marked thereon, at the rates aforesaid, and also correct invoices of the same, and copies of such rates and invoices to the board of war; and clothing purchased on Continental account by the respective States shall be valued, marked, and invoiced in like manner, and copies of such invoices and rates also transmitted to the board of war, and the clothier general. The clothing, so purchased, shall be distributed to and among the sub or State clothiers, to be issued by them to the regimental clothiers, and by the latter, to the officers of the regiments and corps; and the said regimental clothiers shall receive from the officers on delivery of the clothing, the prices thereof so fixed, and they shall every three months settle their accounts of moneys, received for clothing, with the auditors of the army, in which they shall serve, and pay the moneys, which in such settlements shall be found chargeable to them, or in their hands to the paymasters general, or deputy paymasters general of the army or detachment, in which such regimental clothiers shall serve, and the said paymasters general, or deputy paymasters general, shall make returns of the amount of all such moneys so received to the board treasury, that the said paymasters general, or deputy paymasters general may be duly charged with the same; the auditors making such settlements with the regimental clothiers, shall transmit to the paymaster, or deputy paymaster general abstracts of such settlements specifying the balances due from the regimental clothiers respectively, that in case of neglect they may be duly called on for payment of the same.

Copies of such abstracts shall also be transmitted to the board of treasury. Excepting from this rule of distribution all staff officers not taken from the line, who are to receive their clothing immediately from the clothiers general, or if attached to the corps of, or residing in any State at a distance from the clothier general's stores, from the sub clothier of such State, paying for the same at the rates aforesaid, and all moneys so received by the clothier general, or such sub or State clothiers, shall be placed to the credit of the United States, and accounts thereof duly transmitted to the board of treasury. The clothier general to be charged in the settlement of his contingent account, with the moneys so received, and the sub or State clothiers to be accountable for, and pay the moneys received by them to the order of the executive of the State, appointing them respectively, and the State to be charged in its clothing account with the amount of such moneys. excepting also all State officers, who receive commissions on their expenditures of public moneys, who are not to receive any clothing provided at Continental expence.

That all clothing, issued to non commissioned officers and soldiers, enlisted artificers and waggoners, beyound that allowed to them as a county, shall also be valued and paid for at the rate beforementioned, but no non commissioned officer or soldier, waggoner, or artificer, shall be entitled to purchase in any one year out of the public store, any other additional articles than those of hats, hose, shoes, or shirts, and not more of those than are absolutely necessary, and not exceeding the number of the like articles, allowed them in their county clothing.

That all the clothing beforementioned of officers of the line and soldiers shall be issued on returns, certified by the commanding officer of the corps to which they belong, all clothing to the staff officers on the certificates of their principal with the army, or in the district within which they shall serve to artificers on the certificate of the commanding officer of their corps, and two waggoners on the certificate of the quarter master general or of the deputy quarter master general employing them, or of the waggon master general, or deputy waggon master general, under whom they serve.

That no staff officer, artificer or waggoner, not being engaged for at least one year, shall receive clothing, and if any such officer artificer or waggoner, being engaged for one year or more, after receipt of such clothing shall quiet the service before the expiration of the term for which he or they are or shall be engaged, he or they shall forfeit and pay the full value of such clothing, and be subject to all other penalties and inconveniences attending his or their breach of contract or desertion.

Nov. 26, 1779.

Resolved, That the returns for clothing for officers in the medical staffs; regimental surgeons and their mates, who are to draw with the regimental staff excepted, by the director general, or the Physician general, or the surgeon of the district, and such clothing shall be delivered either by the clothier general, or any sub clothier in the state in which the officer to receive clothing shall reside, as is provided in the cases of other staff officers not taken from the line.

That no clothing shall be sold or delivered to non commissioned officers or soldiers beyond the articles they have received as their bounty clothing, it being the intention hereof that surplus only shall be disposed of.

(Extract from the minutes).

CHARLES THOMPSON, *Secretary.*

In Congress, Sept. 6, 1777.

The committee on the Treasury having into consideration the letter from General Gates of 28 Aug., respecting clothing for the army under his command, referred to them by Congress;

Report: That it appears from the clothier general's report, that he has ordered considerable supplies of clothing to be forwarded to the army in the northern department from Boston, and that he has little doubt of being able to furnish in the course of the year, the specific articles of clothing directed to be given as a bounty to the troops, and as it will be equally disadvantageous to the soldiers and the service, should they receive money instead of such clothing; the board disapproves of the stoppages made by the deputy paymaster general, in the northern department, on account of clothing, and directs the money to be returned, except in cases where a regiment has been furnished with more clothing then the bounty.

That the greatest care ought to be taken to do justice to the soldiers, as well as the public in this essential article; it is not sufficient in the opinion of this board that the clothier general charge the regiments with the articles delivered and take receipts of the colonel or commanding officer on delivering the clothing to the captain, or commanding officer of each company, and takes his receipt; each commanding officer of a company ought moreover to be strictly required to keep a clothing account with his company, distinguishing the several articles delivered to each non commissioned officer and private, and taking receipts for the same as his vouchers, and when each non commissioned officer and private respectively shall have received his bounty of clothing, the commanding officer of the company to which he belongs, shall deliver the account and receipts to the commanding officer of the regiment, to enable him to settle the clothing accounts with the clothier general as well as to discover whether equal justice has been done to the company.

That such troops as have not been supplied with clothing ought to be furnished their full bounty without delay, which the board have earnestly recommended to the attention of the clothier general, and he, on his part, has engaged to exert every means in his power to accomplish.

That such of the troops as at their own expense have provided themselves with any of the articles of clothing allowed in bounty, or shall not draw their clothing in the course of the year, shall be entitled to receive the full value thereof at the averaged prices which the clothing of the army shall cost the publick.

And whereas when the bounty of clothing was provided by Congress, it was conceived that it might be impracticable to obtain a sufficient quantity of clothing for regimental coats for the troops, and for that reason two hunting-shirts were substituted, but in the event so considerable has been procured, that the clothier general has been enabled to furnish most of the troops with regimental coats instead of hunting-shirts, and experience having shown that a further alteration of the articles of clothing allowed as a bounty, may be made to the advantage of the soldiers, and without loss to the publick, therefore it is the opinion of the committee that it be,

Resolved, That the clothier general be directed, as far as he shall have it in his power, to furnish all the non commissioned officers and privates, in the service of the United States who have not received their bounty of clothing, at their election, either with the several articles allowed by Congress, in the resolution of the 8th of October, 1776, or in lieu thereof the following articles, viz:

1 regimental coat averaged at	88 & 60-90ths.
1 jacket without sleeves,	2 & 60
1 pair buckskin and 2 pair linen or woolen breeches,	8
1 hat or leathern cap,	2 & 60
2 shirts,	8
1 hunting shirt,	4
2 pair of overalls,	6
2 pair of stockings,	4
2 pair of shoes,	6
1 blanket,	6
Total estimated cost,	856

But as the cost of the articles last specified exceed that of the clothing allowed as a bounty to the troops, by eight dollars and 30 90ths of a dollar, so much shall be stopped out of the pay of every non commissioned officer and private, who shall be supplied in the manner last directed, as will make the amount of clothing he shall receive, equal to the value of the bounty of clothing, which upon an average of the prices of the several articles, is estimated at forty-seven dollars, and 60 90ths of a dollar.

The said report being twice read, on the question put,

Resolved, That Congress agree to the foregoing report and resolves.

By order of Congress.
[Fac simile.] JOHN HANCOCK, *President*.

General Orders, May 20th, 1779.

In all future draughts of clothing, the regimental clothier is to be furnished by the officers commanding companies with returns specifying the men's names, and the particular wants of each. These he is to digest into a regimental return, which being examined and signed by the officer commanding the regiment, and countersigned by himself, with a receipt upon it for the supplies delivered to the regiment, is to be lodged with the clothier general of issues, as a voucher for the delivery.

(Extract from General Orders).

ALEXANDER SCAMMELL, *Adjt. Gen.*

Ordinance for regulating the Clothing Department, for the Armies of the United States.

In Congress, March 23, 1779.

There shall be a clothier general, a sub or State clothier for each State and a regimental clothier.

The clothier general is to be subject to the orders of the board of war and commander in chief.

He is to furnish estimates of the supplies wanted for the army. To apply to the commander in chief and board of war for assistance therein, and to make returns of such estimates to them respectively.

To receive all supplies imported from abroad and purchased in the country by Continental agents.

To superintend the distribution thereof to the State clothiers, to settle accounts with them at least every six months, to keep regular accounts of all the clothing he shall receive, as well as the distribution thereof among the State clothiers, and to transmit his accounts twice in every year to the board of treasury, and settle them in the chamber of accounts when required, and generally to take care on the one hand that justice is done to the public, and on the other that the army receive whatever shall be allowed to them in a direct and seasonable manner, and at the same time so as to act between the Continent and each particular State, that equal and impartial justice may be done on all sides.

The Sub or State Clothier.

A sub or State clothier is to be appointed by each State respectively, to reside with or near the army, or sub detachments thereof; in which the troops of such State may be, as the commander in chief shall direct, the better to know and supply their wants.

The State appointing him is to answerable for his conduct; in case of neglect or misbehavour, he is to be displaced by the commander in chief, and his successor to be appointed by the State to which he belonged. He is to receive of the clothier general, the proportion of clothing assigned for the troops of his State out of the publick clothing imported, or purchased by Continental agents, and from the State for which he is appointed, all the clothing which may at Continental expence be purchased in such States of the latter, their quality and price. He shall transmit correct accounts to the clothier general, and when required, submit the several articles to the inspection of the clothier general, or any person for that purpose deputed by him. He is to issue all clothing, supplies as aforesaid to the regimental clothiers, on returns signed by the commanding officer of the regiments. He is to keep exact returns with each regiment, inspect those of the regimental clothiers, see the articles delivered them duly issued to the troops; and that all the clothing procured at Continental expence, above the allowance made by Congress, drawn by non commissioned officers and privates be charged to them, and credited to the pay rolls; and that the commissioned officers receive what is credited to them and no more.

He is to keep each account with the clothier general, in behalf of the publick, charging the United States only with what is allowed to the officers and men.

Whenever the troops of any State shall have received their proportion of clothing from the Continental store, the supplies purchased at Continental expence, by the State to which they belong, or from both, and there shall remain a surplus which may be wanted for other troops not fully supplied, the sub clothier possessed thereof is to deliver over the supplies to such other State clothiers as the clothier general shall direct, taking duplicate invoices and receipts from the State clothier, to whom they shall be transferred, one set of which he is to deposit with the clothier general, and the other to retain as his own voucher. The clothier general on his part making proper entries in his accounts, to do justice to all concerned.

When from a difficiency in the publick stores, the troops of any State shall not have received their allowance of clothing, the State clothier, without delay, shall represent their wants particularly enumerated in a return for that purpose, to the executive authority of the State to which he belongs, requesting a speedy and adequate supply.

And in case a State shall at its own expence, give and deposit with him any clothing for the more comfortable subsistance of its quota of troops, in addition to the allowance, made by Congress, he is strictly to pursue the directions of such State, as well with respect to the distribution, as for the vouchers for the delivery, and manner and time of settling his accounts, transmitting once in every six months, a copy of such accounts to the clothier general, and as often and whenever required, to the State to which he belongs.

The Regimental Clothier.

The office of the regimental clothier shall always be executed by the regimental paymaster.

He is to be furnished by the captains with returns specifying the men's names, and the particular wants of each. These he is to digest into a regimental return, which being signed by the officer commanding the regiments, and countersigned by himself with a receipt upon it for the supplies delivered the regiment, is to be lodged with the State clothier, and become to him a voucher for the delivery in his settlement with the clothier general.

He is to keep an account with each officer and soldier for every article delivered, taking a receipt from them as his voucher for the delivery.

He is to credit them for the Continental allowance, and to charge them for everything they receive, making stoppages in the monthly pay rolls for whatever they may fall in debt to the publick beyond the allowance. And to prevent any future unequal distribution of clothing, either to the officers or soldiers, and the confusion and complaints, which have heretofore been occasioned in irregular applications by the commanding officers of regiments, to publick agents at different posts, it is hereby strictly enjoined on those agents of the clothier general, and the sub or state clothiers, to issue no clothing on any pretence whatever, but in the manner before prescribed, nor shall any article be credited to either of them on settlement of their accounts, which is not so issued and vouched.

And whereas, often changes of the uniform of regiments have proved inconvenient and expensive, the commander in chief is therefore hereby authorized and directed according to the circumstances of supplies of clothing to fix and prescribe the uniform, as well to regard the colour of facings, as the cut and fashion of the clothes to be worn by the troops of the respective States and regiments, which shall as far as possible be complied with by all purchasing agents employed by Congress, as well as particular states, by the clothier general, sub or State clothier, and regimental clothiers, and all officers and soldiers in the armies of the United States, and when materials can be purchased instead of ready made clothes, it shall always be prefered, in order that they may be made up by the tailors of the several regiments, to save expence, and to save the disadvantages which the soldiers frequently suffer from their unfitness; and instead of breeches, woolen over-alls for the winter and linen for the summer are to be substituted.

(Extract from general orders).

ALEX^R SCAMMEL,

Adjt Genl.

In Congress, March 10, 1780.

For the better regulating the payment of arrears due or to become due to the soldiers for clothing pursuant to the resolution of Congress of 19th Aug. last.

Resolved, That the several regimental paymasters at the end of each year make out returns of clothing drawn by each soldier in the regiment to which he belongs in the course thereof, and of the articles still due, and to be paid for at the value fixed by the clothier general.

That each of the said returns certified by the sub or State clothier of the state to which the regiment may belong and accompanied by a certified copy of the last muster roll, be delivered to the auditors of the army in which the said regiment may be, who shall compare the returns with the muster rolls, file them in the office and report a warrant in the usual form for the sum necessary to discharge the arrears to the soldiers present, and when any part of the regiment happen to be on detachment at that time the sum necessary to pay them, shall, when they return, be granted on a certificate of the inspector who musters the regiment, and settle in the same manner as arrears do to the present.

That each regimental paymaster within two weeks after the receipt of the money, pay off the several companies, and take receipts of the soldiers respectively, to be produced as his vouchers to the auditors at his next settlement of his regimental pay roll.

That the said auditors examine and settle the said accounts and that the balance, if any, which may remain in the hands of the said paymaster by reason of casualties in the regiment, after the taking of the muster rolls as afore said be refunded as directed by a resolution of Congress of the 6th of February, 1778.

That the arrears of clothing due to prisoners, or the legal representatives of such as from time to time have died in the service, be paid for in the manner directed in similar cases as arrears of pay, by the said last resolve recited.

Resolved, That no allowance of pay, rations or subsistance, ought to be made to any person after he ceases to be in office.

That if any issuer deliver out public stores to such persons without being authorized by a resolution of Congress, the same ought to be charged to his account.

(Extract from the minutes.)

CHARLES THOMPSON.
Secretary.

By the United States in Congress assembled, June 18, 1781.

The committee to whom was recommitted their report on the clothier's department, together with the letter of J. Moylan, clothier general, delivered in a report which was taken into consideration and thereupon

Resolved, That all State purchasers of clothing on Continental account, and all State appointments and regulations in the clothing department on Continental account be abolished on the first day of September, at or before which time the sub and agent clothiers, are to deliver to the clothier general all clothing purchased at Continental expence, which they may then have on hand, taking his receipt therefor, a duplicate whereof to be transmitted to the treasury office.

Resolved, That the clothier general in the month of June annually make and deliver into the board of war an estimate of clothing and disbursments for clothing for a year from the first of November then next, that Congress may be enabled to furnish the proper sums, and adopt the necessary measures for procuring the same.

That all non commissioned officers and soldiers who are, or may hereafter be enlisted during the war be annually furnished with : 1 regimental coat full made; 1 pair of cloth breeches ; 1 cloth vest ; 1 pair woolen overalls ; 2 pairs woolen hose ; 2 pairs woolen socks ; 1 felt hat or leathern cap ; 4 shirts ; 2 pairs linen overalls ; 4 pairs strong shoes ; 1 blanket ; 1 rifle shirt ; 1 pair woolen gloves ; 2 pair shoe buckles and one clasp, for stock every two years. That dragoons to receive two pairs of boots, and one pair of spurs, instead of the shoes and buckles annually, also a horseman's cloak every two years.

That the commander in chief and the general commanding

in a separate department respectively be, and hereby are authorized to direct whatever clothing shall from time to time be dealt out to sub officers and waggoners, having regard to the nature of their service, and the terms of their contract, and time for which they are engaged.

That summer clothing be ready to be issued on the 15th day of April annually, and the winter clothing on the 1st day of November following, and be delivered at such time as the commander in chief, or the commanding general in a separate department shall direct.

That the clothier general deals out the clothing regimentally, and keep regular accounts against the respective regimental clothiers, taking care to have the clothing equally and impartially distributed, when it is found incompetent for the whole army.

That previous to the day of issue the regimental clothiers settle their accounts with the clothier general and receive his certificates of the arrearages of clothing due to their respective regiments, and present him with a return of the number of men for whom clothing is to be drawn on the day of general issue, the said return to be examined and certified by the officers commanding their respective regiments, and signed by the brigadier or officer commanding the brigade.

That all extra issues to detachments for accidental loss of clothing, be by certificates of the commanding officer of the regiment or detachment to which the non commissioned officers or soldiers in whose behalf such applications are made shall belong, the said certificates being approved and signed by the commander in chief or commanding general of a separate army.

That all issues of clothing be made from the magazines or places of general issues with the army to avoid the necessity of detached issues, the officers commanding parties or detachments are to be answerable that they are supplied, so far as may be, from the magazines or stores at camp previous to their leaving the army to which they belong.

That no article of clothing be issued by the clothier general, his deputy or assistants, but by returns of certificates made and approved as aforesaid.

That no non commissioned officer or soldier who is not engaged during war, or for the term at least of one year, to be furnished with any article of clothing.

That the clothier general from time to time notify the paymaster general of all surplusages of clothing, specifying the corps to which they belong, that stoppages may be made therefor.

That he make return to the board of war of all clothing on hand and persons employed in the department, with the wages given to each, regularly once in two months.

That the quarter master general and his deputies in the several States, shall, on the requisition of the clothier general, furnish the means of transportation of all articles of clothing from the place where imported, received, or purchased, to the place of deposit, and a careful waggon master or conductor to be appointed by the quarter master general, or some of his deputies shall proceed with the clothing who shall be answerable for all deficiencies on the road, unless they shall be able to show that the same happened by unavoidable accident, and not through misconduct or want of attention.

That in case of injuries or deficiencies happening in the transportation of clothing, the clothier stationed at the magazine or place of the deposit shall represent the matter to the nearest commanding officer of the troops of the United States, that the waggon master or conductor having had charge of the clothing so damaged or deficient, may be tried by a court martial, and if found guilty compelled to restore the goods lost or their value, or make satisfaction for damages that accrued through his neglect or mismanagement, or to be punished according to the nature of his offence by judgment of a court martial.

That the clothier general have the management, direction and superintendence of hides, subject to the orders of the board of war, with full power to call for proper returns from such persons as have heretofore had the management of hides.

That all commissaries make monthly returns to the clothier

general of the hides on hand, and the commissary general make monthly returns to him of all the live cattle delivered over to the commissaries of the army.

That the quarter master or his deputy, on the application of the clothier general or either of his deputies, furnish waggons for transporting raw or manufactured hides, to such places as they shall direct.

That the clothier general, with concurrence of the superintendents of finance be authorized to appoint such number of persons, to transact the business of the clothing department during this present campaign, as they may find necessary from time and to ascertain their wages.

That the clothier general make monthly returns to the commander in chief.

That resolutions heretofore passed respecting the clothing and hide department, inconsistent with this arrangement, and the resolutions now passed, be and are hereby repealed.

THE HISTORY OF THE REGIMENT CONCLUDED.

With the termination of Lieutenant Blake's journal we are left without any direct record of the doings of the regiment, and shall be only able to follow its campaigns and privations by the general history of the army of which it formed a part, and we commence anew with January 1st, 1781. The new year opened with a deep gloom, the whole army, north as well as south, was suffering severely both for clothing and provisions. The winter was unusually severe, the soldiers were often on the point of starvation, and were for days without meat, and nearly all the time on short allowance, while most of them had received no pay for about a year. As for clothing they were often so destitute that many of them could not do guard duty without borrowing from their comrades, while for shoes they were still more deficient, and parties who were on fatigue duty for firewood and forage could often be tracked by the blood from their bruised feet.

The writer remembers hearing an old soldier of this regiment relate that having at this period received a furlough to visit his home, he had to remain two days in camp to make a pair of pantaloons and a pair of moccasins out of his old blanket before he could start on his long journey. It was during this hard winter that the Pennsylvania line mutinied, and were soon joined by the New Jersey troops. This alarming affair was partially settled by the more patient and faithful eastern troops being led against them, by which they were overawed, and supplies were afterwards wrung from the unwilling farmers and holders by military orders, and the wants of the army better supplied.

It was at this period that Gen. Washington addressed a pressing letter to President Weare of New Hampshire, earnestly urging that state to make some exertions to relieve the distresses of the army. A circular to the same effect was sent to all the New England states, and was confided to Gen. Knox as a special agent to inforce the appeal. To President Weare Washington plainly wrote: "I give it decidedly as my opinion that it is vain to think that an army can be kept together much longer under such a variety of sufferings as ours has experienced, and that unless some immediate and spirited measures are adopted to furnish at least three months' pay to the troops in money that will be of some value to them, and at the same time provide means to clothe and feed them better than they have been, the worst that can befall us may be expected."

"The legislatures of New Hampshire and Massachusetts nobly responded," says Sparks, "to this call, and immediately voted a gratuity of twenty-four dollars in hard money to each of the noncommissioned officers and soldiers belonging to those states who were engaged to serve for the war."

During the ensuing summer the military operations were active and important, in many of which this regiment bore a full share. But by far the most important was the great march to Virginia and the capture of Cornwallis and his whole army at Yorktown.

I have not been able to give any detailed account of the doings of the New Hampshire regiments in the great strategic marches and movements, or in the battles which resulted in this great victory and the consequences that followed from it.

The war culminated then and it mainly closed the battles of the Revolution. Here the regiment met with a great loss in the death of its commander,

Alexander Scammell. He was appointed in 1777, colonel of the Third New Hampshire regiment, which belonged to the same brigade as the other two; and when on the 1st of January, 1781, his regiment and the Second were merged in the First, he succeeded Col. Cilley as commander. He had the year previous been adjutant general of the army, but early in this year, took command of the regiment. At the time he was captured he was acting officer of the day. A monument was erected to his memory at Williamsburg on which was the following inscription, written by his friend Col. Humphreys:

ALEXANDER SCAMMELL,

Adjutant general of the American armies, and colonel of the First New Hampshire regiment, while he commanded a chosen corp of light infantry, at the successful siege of Yorktown in Virginia, was in the gallant performance of his duty as field officer of the day, unfortunately captured and afterwards insidiously wounded, of which wound he expired at Williamsburg, Oct. 6, 1781.

In the autumn of this year we find the regiment returned to the banks of the Hudson, under the command of Lt. Col. Dearborn, while its first colonel was now a brigadier in the line and the commanding general.

It was designed to send the two New Hampshire regiments up the Mohawk to relieve Col. Willet's troops, whose time had expired.

On December 5th they were waiting to receive clothing which was to be forwarded by the great financier, Robert Morris.

On the 12th Gen. Stark wrote to Gen. Heath as follows :

"I am sorry to hear that any troops suffer more than these in this quarter (our enemies excepted), but since some are more wretched we must submit to our fate like good soldiers. I am sure it is not practicable for the troops that are here to go to the Mohawk river until they are clothed. Indeed I am obliged to detain the six months' men to do the necessary camp duty on account of the nakedness of the Continental troops.

"In the last duty report, only thirty-six 'three years and during the war' men, including sergeants, were fit for duty in the two regiments. The remainder are so naked that they cannot procure fuel for their own use.

"If there is a possibility of sending some blankets, shirts, overalls, stockings and shoes, they might afford a temporary relief, and I dare say they would prove satisfactory.

"My predictions in my last were realized, on the evening of the 10th instant the troops mutinied, but by seasonable interposition of the officers it was quelled very easily.

"But this may be but a prelude to an insurrection of a more serious nature."

About this time Gen. Heath writes to Gen. Stark:

" The soldiers will receive ample supplies of clothing, but it will be late before it is all ready. The paymasters of the New Hampshire regiments have drawn shoes, hose and some overalls, shirts, etc., for the most necessitous men. These will be conveyed to Albany in a few days when all the detachments will join their corps."

The regiment wintered in detachments at Saratoga, Schenectady and the neighboring posts. At this time the difficulties between New York and Vermont were at their height and a condition little short of actual war existed between them, while Gen. Stark thought New Hampshire ought to settle the difficulty by claiming the territory it had formerly granted and holding it.

In April, 1782, Washington established his head quarters at Newburg, where he continued most of the time, till nearly all the army was discharged.

In the autumn the army, which had mainly all been encamped at Verplanck's point, marched up and was hutted at New Windsor, two miles below Washington's quarters, and here or in the neighborhood our regiment spent the winter of 1782 and the following year.

These were months of repose, the war was over, their long weary marches and months of privations were past, the battles had been fought, the great cause for which they had so long contended was gained, and they could look forward to peace and prosperity.

But the definitive treaty had not been signed, and the British army still held New York. Under these circumstances Washington recommended that the army should still be retained, and so they remained till November, when the British commander notified Washington that he was ready to evacuate the city of New York, which he soon did, and Washington entered it the same day, and during that month nearly all of our troops were disbanded.

But for some reason the First New Hampshire regiment, which had long before included the remaining officers and soldiers of the Second and Third, and was, therefore, the sole representative of the New Hampshire line, remained. Why they should have been the last, or at least among the very last, to lay down their arms we are not able to state. The pay rolls show that they were encamped on the Hudson at or near New Windsor during the month of December, 1783, and there is but little doubt they were disbanded January 1st, 1784; and assuming that it was a continuous corps from April, 1775, it shows a *service of eight years and eight months.* Can any other regiment from any state show so long a record? A regiment is always a changing body, and usually a diminishing one, and we cannot expect to find more than a few names on the last roll to correspond with the first one: still there are a few among the officers, and more among the men who could say they had followed its fortunes from its inception to its close.

I find that during the last two years, and after war was mainly over, many new names of officers are found on the rolls. These were no doubt from the Second regiment who, with the enlisted men, were transferred to the First. Lt. Col. Dearborn must have retired from the command early in the spring of 1783, for Major Scott was acting commander in March and Lt. Col. Reid in May, and he continued till the end of that year. During one of the last years of the war, while the New Hampshire forces were encamped at New Windsor, the New York troops received a grant of land from the legislature of that state. When the New Hampshire forces caused a petition to be drawn up to that legislature asking for a similar grant, for the reason that they had done as much as their own soldiers for the defense of New York, and was equally deserving of land, of which the state had an abundance while their own state had none, the signers were very numerous, Gen. Stark being at the head; but they did not obtain their object. The document is, or was, to be found among the Schuyler papers.

It has often been asserted that many of the officers and soldiers of the revolution were paid in a depreciated currency and so never received what they were entitled to. A close examination of Paymaster Blake's records will show that this statement, so far as this regiment was concerned, is incorrect. It is true that between January, 1777 and July, 1781, the currency depreciated from par to nearly nothing, and during the three years first named, much of the payments must have been in this currency; but in 1781 the legislature passed an act to equalize the depreciation for each month. The rolls with the allowances is still extant, with the sums due each man, to make the pay he received equal to good money, and after this period they were paid in hard money or government certificates; but these were often disposed of at a large discount, though a large part of the community suffered in this depreciation as well as the soldiers. In consequence of the great demand for men during the war to fill the quota assigned to the towns they often paid large sums, sometimes in silver, to the enlisting soldiers, and when we consider the gratuities paid by the states and the pensions granted by the act of 1818, and subsequently, we must allow that, considering the condition of the country and the almost universal sufferings of all classes during and after the revolution, the soldiers, as a class, could not complain.

The scale of depreciation before referred to may be useful for reference, and is given on the next page. It will be seen that in January, 1777, it was worth nearly par with silver; in something over four years it had reached nearly to zero. It is a curious fact that a comparison of the money issued by the late rebel government shows its rate of depreciation was very similar, and reached the same value in just about the same time.

Scale of Depreciation.

	1777.	1778.	1779.	1780.	1781.
January,	£104	£325	£742	£2934	£7500
February,	110	350	868	3322	7500
March,	106	375	1000	3739	7500
April,	110	400	1104	4000	7500
May,	114	400	1215	4800	7500
June,	120	425	1342	5700	12000
July,	125	450	1477	6000	
August,	150	475	1630	6300	
September,	175	500	1800	6500	
October,	275	545	2030	6700	
November,	300	634	2308	7000	
December,	310	620	2393	7300	

It may be interesting to many to know the arrangement and numbers that constituted a regiment, and how the rank and pay of the officers compared with those of the present day. To do this we compile and print some of the paymasters' reports at different times as examples. This shows that the field officers had each a company. This is still the practice in the English army, where a general has a regiment commanded by a lieutenant colonel, and the lieutenant colonel a company, etc. This is for the purpose of drawing the pay of a subaltern officer in addition to their own; but in this regiment they do not seem to have received additional pay, and after 1781 the form seems to have been abandoned. At one period one of the companies were styled a light infantry company. There were some half ranks, as we occasionally meet with a "captain lieutenant" and occasionally "second lieutenant" which did not correspond to ensign.

The subjoined list shows the number of companies and men, with the names of their commanders during 1780 and 1782:

Abstract of the Roll of the First New Hampshire Regiment, for 1780.

	No. of Men.
Colonel's company, Capt. Simon Sortwell	47
Lieutenant colonel's company, Lieut. Daniel Clapp, comd'g	37
Major's company, Capt. Moody Dustin	46
Capt. Amos Morrell's company	57
Capt. Jason Wait's company	42
Capt. Amos Emerson's company	39
Capt. Ebenezer Frye's company	41
Capt. Isaac Farwell's company	40
Capt. Nathaniel Hutchin's company	45
Whole number of enlisted men	394

During the year 1782 there were nine companies, viz:

		Enlisted Men.
No. one was commanded by Capt. Josiah Munroe, had		62
No. two " " by Capt. Ebenezer Frye		60
No. three " " by Capt. Isaac Farwell		56
No. four " " by Capt. Daniel Livermore		53
No. five " " by Capt. Isaac Frye		57
No. six " " by Capt. Asa Senter		56
No. seven " " by Capt. Moody Dustin		52
No. eight " " by Capt. Jona. Cass		50
No. nine " " by Capt. Benj. Ellis		56
		502

These numbers constitute all whose names were borne on the roll for the year. Of those a few died, some deserted, and some were discharged. Against these were some joining in every month, particularly during the months of April and July. So it is doubtful if there were at any time four hundred and fifty effective men. There were nine captains, nine lieutenants and one ensign on the rolls during that year.

A List of the Names of the Field, Staff and other Commissioned Officers in the First New Hampshire Regiment under my Command, with the several Casualties and Promotions that has happened in the course of the year 1780.

APPOINTED.	OFFICERS' NAMES.	RANK.	REMARKS.
Feb. 22, 1777,...	Joseph Cilley,............	Colonel.........	
Sept. 20, 1777,...	Jeremiah Gilman,......	Lieut. Colonel.	Resigned March 24, 1780.
March 24, 1780,..	Benjamin Titcomb,.....	Lieut. Colonel, ...	Deranged. Jan. 1, 1781.
Sept. 20, 1777,..	William Scott,.........	Major..........	
May 2, 1777,......	John Hale, ...	Surgeon,........	Resigned Jan. 11, 1780.
June 28, 1780,..	Nathaniel Gardiner,...	Surgeon,........	Resigned Dec. 17, 1782.
May 22, 1777,...	Jonathan Pool..........	Surgeon's Mate,....	Resigned June 11, 1780.
Jan. 1, 1778,....	Jeremiah Pritchard,...	Lieut. and Adjt.,..	Resigned July 5, 1780.
Sept. 20, 1777,..	Joseph Mills...........	Ens. and Adjt.,....	Ap. Adjt. May 1. 1780, Lt. July 5, 1780.
Aug. 23, 1778,..	Josiah Munro,.........	Lieut. and Q. M....	Resigned Q. M. July 5, a Captain July 5.
Aug. 24, 1779,..	Jona Willard,.........	Lieut. and Q. M....	Appointed July 5.
March 25, 1780,.	Thomas Blake,........	Lieut. and Pay Mr.	August 24, 1779.
Nov. 8, 1776,....	Amos Morrill,..........	Captain,.........	Promoted to Major and trans. to 2d Reg.
Nov. 8, 1776,....	Jason Wait.............	Captain,.........	Promoted to Major and trans. to 3d Reg.
Nov. 8, 1776,....	Amos Emerson,........	Captain,.........	Resigned March 24, 1780.
Nov. 8, 1776,....	Ebenezer Frye,.........	Captain,.........	[Cashiered Dec. 6, 1782.]
Nov. 8, 1776,....	Isaac Farwell..........	Captain,.........	
April 3, 1777,...	Nathaniel Hutchins,...	Captain..........	
Sept. 20, 1777,..	Simon Sartwell,........	Captain. Lieut.,..	A Captain March 25, 1780.
March 5, 1778,..	Moody Dustin,........	Lieutenant,.....	Promoted to Captain March 25, 1780.

Date	Name	Rank	Remarks
Nov. 8, 1776,	Daniel Clapp,	Lieutenant,	Promoted to Captain. Lieut. July 5, 1780.
Nov. 8, 1776,	Asa Senter,	Lieutenant,	Promoted to Captain 1781.
Nov. 8, 1776,	Bezaleel Howe,	Lieutenant,	
Sept. 20, 1777,	Simon Morrill,	Lieutenant,	Resigned May 20, 1780.
March 5, 1778,	Joshua Thompson,	Lieutenant,	
July 19, 1777,	Jona Perkins,	Ensign,	Promoted to Lieutenant March 25, 1780.
Sept. 28, 1778,	Hubbard Carter,	Ensign,	Promoted to a Lieutenant July 5, 1780.
Jan. 10, 1778,	Samuel Thompson,	Ensign,	On furlough.

I do hereby certify that the above list is a true state and other occurrences that have happened to the Staff, Field, and other Officers in the Regiment under my Command during the year 1780, to the best of my knowledge.

New Hampshire Village [on the Hudson,]
Dec. 31, 1780.

JOSEPH CILLEY, Col°,
Pr. JOSIAH GILLMAN, Jun'.

The above is inserted as a specimen of the annual return which every commander was obliged to make of the changes occurring during the year, as well as the date of the appointment of each officer.

To this may be added the following which will complete the list from the fall of 1776 to December, 1781.

APPOINTED.	OFFICERS' NAMES.	RANK.	REMARKS.
Nov. 8, 1776.	Benjamin Kimball.	Lt. & Paymaster.	Killed Aug. 23, 1779.
March 8, 1781.	John Adams.	Ensign.	A Lieut. Oct., 1781.
June 1, 1779.	Robert Barnet.	Lieutenant.	Resigned Dec., 1780.
Jan. 1, 1777.	James Gould.	Lieutenant.	Retired in 1778.
Jan. 1, 1777.	Nathaniel McCauley.	Lieutenant.	Killed Aug. 31st, 1779.
Jan. 1, 1777.	Caleb Stark.	Adjutant.	Resigned June, 1778.
Jan. 1, 1777.	William Lee.	Lieutenant.	Resigned Jan., 1778.
Jan. 1, 1777.	Joseph Lawrence.	Ensign.	Died June 4, 1777.
Jan. 1, 1777.	James Taggart.	Lieutenant.	Resigned Aug. 1778.
Jan. 1, 1777.	Patrick Cogan.	Qr. Master.	Died Aug., 1778.
Jan. 1, 1777.	John Joiner.	Qr. Master Sergt.	Discharged, 1779.
Jan. 1, 1777.	Samuel Caldwell.	Sergt. Major.	Discharged, 1780.
Jan. 1, 1777.	James Campbell.	Drum Major.	Discharged, 1780.

The reader will notice that very few officers belonging to this regiment were killed during the whole war, while by the record, they fought bravely in almost every important battle.

On the roll, dated Dec. 31st, 1782, are to be found the names of the following officers not on the former rolls. Most of them had been transferred from the Third regiment when that was merged in the First and Second regiments.

When Commenced.	Names.	Rank, &c.
Jan. 1, 1781.	Alexander Scammell.	Col. died Oct. 6, 1781.
Jan. 1, 1781.	Henry Dearborn.......	Lieutenant Colonel.
" " "	Henry Dearborn.......	Lieut. Col. commandant, Oct. 6, 1781.
" " "	Daniel Livermore......	Captain.
" " "	Isaac Frye.	"
" " "	Benjamin Ellis.........	"
May 12, 1781.	Asa Senter............	Capt. promoted.
Jan. 1, 1781,	Archibald Stark.......	Lieutenant.
" " "	Nathan Hoyt.	"
" " "	Jonathan Cass, ...	"
May 11, 1781.	Moses Page............	Ensign.
" " "	Jonathan Cilley, ...	Lieutenant.
" " "	John Harvey, ...	"
" " "	Samuel Wells..........	"
" " "	Nathan Weare,........	"
" " "	Edward Mason,.......	Sergeant Major.
" " "	John Jones.............	Qr. Master Sergt.
" " "	Samuel Judkins.	Drum Major.
" " "	John Scott.	Fife Major.

The following additional names are of persons who served during some part of the year 1783. It is supposed they were transferred from the Second regiment: George Reid, Lieut. Col. commandant; Amos Merrill, Major; James Cass, Major; Samuel Cheny, Captain; Joseph Potter, Captain; Joseph Boynton, Lieutenant; Caleb Blodgett, Lieutenant; James Blanchard, Lieutenant; Lemuel Mason, Lieutenant: Ebenezer Stockton, Surgeon; David Allen, Surgeon's Mate.

ALLOWANCE TO OFFICERS.

" *Dr. The United States*
  To the Officers of the First New Hampshire Regiment.

For subsistence for September, 1783. [this was in lieu of rations.]

To 1 Lieut. Col. commandant & two servants,	$32 00
1 Major and 1 servant,	20 00
5 Captains @ $12,	60 00
8 Subalterns, @ $8,	64 00
1 Surgeon and servant,	16 00
	$192 00

To the above was appended the following as the list of officers. This is the only list I have been able to find for that year, and it is likely that they continued till the regiment was finally disbanded at the close of that year, as it was certainly at or near New Windsor on the Hudson, October, 7th, 1783:

Col. Reid. Lieuts. Boynton,
Maj. Carr, Blodgett,
Capts. Livermore, Howe,
  Frye, Menow,
  Dustin, Thompson,
  Senter, Bacon,
  Potter, Adams.
    Doctor Stockton.

[Col. Dearborn and Maj. Scott had then retired as the war was over.]

FIRST NEW HAMPSHIRE REGIMENT. 87

In an account rendered for the pay of the regiment for Jan., 1783, the following is the number of commissioned and noncommissioned officers allowed for a regiment, as also the then number of privates. From this amount is deducted for deficiency of officers, two lieutenants, nine ensigns, thirteen sergeants, four corporals, four drummers and two hundred and thirty-four privates. So there was in fact only four hundred and forty-eight rank and file in the regiment at that date.

The following shows the pay of officers and men which was not changed during the war:

1 Lieut. Col. commandant, pr month,	$75	
2 Majors at $50.	100	
9 Captains @ $40,	360	
12 Lieuts. @ $26⅔,	320	
9 Ensigns @ $20,	180	
1 Surgeon @	65	
1 do. Mate,	45	
Additional pay of Adjutant and Qr. Masters,	26	
Do. of Pay Master,	30	$1201
1 Sergeant Major and 1 Qr. Master Sergeant @ $10,	20	
1 Drum Major and 1 Fife Major @ $9,	18	
45 Sergeants. @ $10,	450	
27 Corporals @ $7¼,	198¾	
20 Drummers and Fifers @ 7⅓,	146⅔	
585 Privates, @ $6⅔,	3900	
	———	4732⅔
		5933⅔

The following receipts show that the regiment was still in service as late as up to January 1st, 1784. I find no evidence that the regiment was extant at a later period. It was no doubt discharged at that time:

Received of Thomas Blake Pay Master twenty Dollars for the subsistence of myself and one servant for December, 1783.

JAMES CASS, Major.

Received of Thomas Blake twelve Dollars each for our subsistence for December, 1783.

D. LIVERMORE, Capt. MOODY DUSTIN, Capt.
JOS. POTTER, Capt.   ISAAC FRYE, Capt.

There is a similar one for the same month signed by

J. BOYNTON, Adjt.   OLIVER BARRON, Lt.
J. THOMPSON, Lt.   BEZ^L HOWE, Lt.
J. ADAMS, Lt.   T. MORROW, Lt.

Dr.   The United States in account current with the New Hampshire regiment.   Cr.

		(D. fic. price.)	
Amount of pay of the regiment for April, 1783.		By 1 Capt. Act'g Major of Brigade........	$40 00
1 Lt. Col. Commandant........	$75 00	9 Ensigns (Deficient) at $20.........	180 00
2 Majors at $50........	100 00	3 Sergeants Do. at $10........	30 00
9 Captains at $40........	360 00	78 Privates, (Deficient) $6⅔........	520 00
12 Lieutenants at $26⅔........	320 00	2 Do. in N. H. sick, $6⅔........	13 ⅓
9 Ensigns at $20........	180 00		
1 Surgeon........	50 00		
1 S. Mate........	42 00		
Additional pay of Adjutant Qr. Mr........	26 00		
Do. of Pay Master........	30 00		
Sergeant Major and Qr. Mr. Sergeant........	20 00		
Drum and Fife Majors........	18 00		
45 Sergeants at $10........	450 00		
25 Corporals at $7⅓........	198 00		
20 Drummers and Fifers at $7⅓........	146 00		
385 Privates at 6⅔ (standard)........	2000 00		
1 Super-numerary Lt........	26		
5 Do. Corporals 7⅓........	36		
		Amount to balance........	5204 ⅔
	$5988 00		$5988 00

The allowance to officers for subsistence was pr month:
Lt. Col. for self and 2 Servants........ $22 00
Major and Servant........ 20 00
Surgeon and Servant........ 16 00
Captains........ 12 00
Lieutenants........ 8 00

In the last years of the war ensigns were dispensed with.

It will be seen by the above that the minimum standard for a regiment was 585 privates, and when this was deficient the commander only ranked as a lieutenant colonel. Till about 1780 the accounts seem to have been kept in pounds, shillings and pence, and after that in dollars and its fractions.

GENERAL JOHN STARK.

Few officers of the revolution have received so much biographical attention as Gen. Stark, and, although he was often disposed to disregard the arrangements of his superior officers and of his state authorities, he always retained his popularity with his soldiers and the people.

John Stark was born at Londonderry, in New Hampshire, August 28th, 1728. He was the son of Archibald Stark, who was born at Glasgow, in Scotland, in 1697, and received his education at the university in that city. At an early age he removed with his father and family to Londonderry, in Ireland, where he married; and in 1720 he embarked with a company for New Hampshire, where many of his countrymen were then located; and he finally settled a short distance above Amoskeag Falls, in what is now the city of Manchester. He died in 1758.

John Stark resided with his father till he was twenty-four years of age. That region was a frontier, and he was brought up in a school of hardship and exposure. In 1752, while on a branch of the upper Merrimac, he was taken prisoner by the Indians and carried to the St. Francis village, from whence he was ransomed, and returned home. In the French war from 1755 to the conquest of Canada, John Stark was most of the time in service, and as captain of a company of rangers he did deeds of valor that brought praise from the

British officers, where jealousy of the provincials was extreme.

The experience of Stark in the French war had well fitted him to take a leading part in the revolution, and when the doings of the British on the 19th of April, 1775, reached him, he immediately started for the scene of war, calling on the people to volunteer as he proceeded. When he reached Cambridge he had with him a considerable force from his province, many of whom looked to him as their leader. In a few days it was decided to organize these men into regiments, and he was soon at the head of a regiment of fourteen companies. This regiment he led at the battle of Bunker hill, of which he was one of the heroes, and where he won the praise and gratitude of his country. He continued with his regiment near Boston till the evacuation of the British forces in March, 1776. Afterwards he marched to New York and by way of Albany to Canada, where he was for a time in command of Montreal. After the retreat from Canada, his command returned to Crown point and soon after to Ticonderoga, where Col. Stark was in command of a brigade. From this place he marched for Pennsylvania, where he was under the direct command of Washington. Here he contributed to the capture of the Hessians at Princeton, the result of which, happening at a time of great gloom and depression, filled the hearts of the patriots with hope and joy.

As the time for which his regiment had enlisted had previously expired, he, with his regiment, returned to enter at once into the arrangement by his state to raise three regiments for the Continental service for three years, or the war; and he was appointed the commander of the First, while Cols. Poor and Scammell were to command the other two. In March, 1777, the regiment had been organized and part of it on the way to Ticonderoga, while he repaired to Exeter to complete the final arrangements, where he learned that Col. Poor had been promoted to a brigadier, thus being under the command of one he deemed his junior; and taking umbrage at this, he resigned the command of the regiment and returned home. Perhaps this was after all, providential; for when the alarm, consequent on the capture of Ticonderoga came to his state, he was appointed by the legislature to command their troops, and his popularity, no doubt, did much to arouse the people to the necessity of immediate action. Being independent of the control of the Continental officers, he managed things in his own way, and the success at Bennington was the result. He was also in command of a large force from his own state, and assisted in the victory over Burgoyne at Saratoga. As congress had appointed Stark a brigadier in the regular army, he was ordered into service at Albany, and afterwards at West Point, where he was on the court martial which condemned André to death as a spy. In the spring he was in command of the northern department with his head quarters at Saratoga, which he held for that year. During 1782, he was confined at home with the rheumatism, and did not join the army till the spring of 1783. With the close of the war he resigned his commission and returned home, where he died May 8th, 1822. Gen. Stark has been the subject of much biography and almost unlimited praise; and far be it from me to cast any shadow over one so patriotic and brave, and who contributed so much to the glory of his country; but he had his faults. Like many self-reliant men, he was headstrong in the extreme. In his difficulty with Gen. Folsom, as mentioned on another page, he was altogether wrong, as Folsom fairly outranked him, and it was not a time to indulge in a jealous feeling. Again, when Poor was made a brigadier, it was his duty as an officer and a patriot to submit; and when at the close of the war he had drawn the pay of his chaplain and refused to pay it over, and after years of waiting, it could only be recovered by an act of the legislature, it showed he was not guided by a spirit of justice and honor.

In this meagre sketch of one whose whole life would fill a volume, it is only possible to give an outline, which I have drawn mainly from his memoir by his grandson, to which work I would recommend any one desirous of perusing a life of Gen. Stark; and if I have been obliged to criticise his course, it has been done only from a desire to truthfully give very briefly the life of the first commander of the regiment, whose history is now detailed.

COLONEL JOSEPH CILLEY

Was the son of Capt. Joseph Cilley, who was son of Thomas Cilley. He was born at Nottingham, N. H., in 1734. Married in 1756, Sarah Longfellow, daughter of Jonathan Longfellow. They had six sons who lived to manhood. Their names were: Bradbury, Jonathan, Greenleaf, Daniel, Jacob and Horatio Gates; also three daughters, who were married. A grandson of Col. Joseph Cilley (son of Bradbury), is now living in Nottingham. He was an officer in the war of 1812, and was wounded in an engagement. He earned a reputation for energy and bravery, and at the age of eighty, is still (1868), smart, hale and hearty. He has been United States senator, and held other offices. Col. Cilley was one of the zealous patriots who made the attack on Fort William and Mary (Portsmouth harbor), in 1774, and assisted to carry off the cannon and powder.

Upon the news of the battle at Lexington reaching him, he marched from Nottingham for the scene of action at the head of about a hundred volunteers belonging to that town and the vicinity. He was appointed by the legislature of New Hampshire, a major in Col. Poor's regiment. As this regiment was engaged in the defense of their own state, he did not participate in the battle of Bunker hill. When it was decided to form the three regiments of the New Hampshire line, authorized by congress, Col. Stark was appointed to the command of the First, and Maj. Cilley was appointed lieutenant colonel.

This arrangement was made, as the regimental ledger records, Nov. 8th, 1776, but the pay roll shows it was not perfected till Jan. 1st, 1777. It was probable that the winter was employed in recruiting and arranging for active duty in the spring; it is not likely that it marched before the first of May. Early in this year, Col. Stark resigned in consequence of Col. Poor's promotion to a brigadier, and on the 22d of February, Lt. Col. Cilley was appointed colonel of the First New Hampshire regiment in the line. I shall not undertake to give here an account of his marches, campaigns and battles, through which he passed in the following four years, so eventful in the history of our country, as the journal gives the outlines; and the deficiency of papers and documents relating to Col. Cilley and his officers makes any connected account of their personal history impossible; but I gather from various sources sufficient to show that he proved a brave, patriotic and efficient officer, always prompt to duty, careful of his men, and winning the approbation of his commanders, as also the confidence of his own officers and soldiers. The following accounts of Col. Cilley and his son are mainly taken from printed works, and are, no doubt, perfectly reliable:

When Col. Cilley marched from home he took with him his second son, Jonathan, who was probably less than fifteen years old. This was very common at

that time, and, no doubt, was often found very useful.
When the sudden march from Ticonderoga took place
this young man was taken prisoner; and, as he was a
mere boy, the captor learning who he was, took him to
Gen. Burgoyne, who ordered that he should be treated
kindly, and provided with a pass to join his father.
He also ordered that he might select from the captured
baggage of the Americans, which was immense, any
articles of clothing he might wish. He therefore took
the best looking coat he could find. It proved to belong
to Maj. Hull (afterwards the celebrated Gen. Hull).
He was also furnished with an old horse and a pair of
saddle bags filled with Burgoyne's proclamations to
convey to his father. On reaching the regiment, he
found it on parade, with his father in front. The
colonel seized one of the proclamations, and having
read it, ordered them all to be torn in pieces, and said,
"Thus will the British army be scattered." During this
same disastrous retreat, at night, when everything was
in confusion, Gen. Kosciusko, not being able to find
his own horse, took the first that came in his way. It
belonged to Adjutant Stark, who, not finding his horse
where he left it, proceeded on foot till daylight, when
he discovered the Polish general mounted upon his
horse and demanded his property, which the other
refused to give up. Kosciusko was very impulsive,
and high words ensued. The adjutant demanded satisfaction, while the general replied, that "a subaltern is
not of sufficient rank to meet a brigadier general."

"If he is not," said a person coming up on foot, "I am. This officer is, general, my adjutant, the horse is his property, and his demand is a proper one." "Ah, Col. Cilley," replied the general, "if that is the case I will give up the horse." The adjutant recovered his horse; but in half an hour afterward, Col. Cilley, who had lost his own horse, said, "Stark, I am tired, you must lend me your horse," which was of course complied with. The retreat from Ticonderoga, and the summer campaign on the upper part of the Hudson river, was a trying time to the regiment and its officers. The great battle which resulted in the capture of Burgoyne and his army took place on the 17th of October; here Col. Cilley distinguished himself, and received the thanks of his commanding general. The part which Col. C. took in this battle will be noticed in the doings of the regiment on that eventful day, as also in the battle of Monmouth, Stony point, and others.

As the three regiments, comprising the New Hampshire line, had, by casualties and other causes resulting from active service in the field, become much diminished, congress ordered that the three regiments should, on the 1st of June, 1781, be merged into two, and the excess of officers caused by this arrangement should be "deranged," a military term perhaps meaning retired. How the lot to retire should have fallen to Col. Cilley is not known, but perhaps his regiment was then less in number than either of the others, and so his retirement became necessary. His name on the roll ceases from this date, and that of Alexander Scammell appears as his successor, to meet a glorious death after commanding the regiment for about nine months. On leaving his command, he returned to enjoy the comforts of home, after an absence of over five and a half years. It is not likely that Col. Cilley was again in active service during the war, and the anecdote of his punishing a British officer who had insulted him in New York, after peace, as stated in the *Life of Stark*, p. 337, is no doubt erroneous.

The following is the only letter I have been able to find from Col. Cilley. It shows that he was then residing at his home, and I think had been there since Jan., 1781:

"NOTTINGHAM, June 9, 1783.

"Dear Sir: As I understand that you are to be settled within camp by the paymaster general, I suppose that the returned rations for the year '80, will also be settled. If so I shall be greatly obliged to you to settle mine as the rest is settled and deliver the same to Lt. Cilley who will give you a receipt for the same. As to news we have none here, only the glorious news of peace. All our money has vanished and there is the greatest cry for money and corn that I have seen in my day but I hope for better times. My best compliments to all the gentlemen of your line. With due respect I am sir,

"Your humble servant,
"Jos. CILLEY.

"To Lt. Thomas Blake,
"Pay Master to the New Hampshire Regiment,
"New Winsor, N. Y."

On the 22d of June, 1786, he was appointed first major general of the New Hampshire militia, and also served the state in various civil capacities. Previous to the war he had been a self-made lawyer and was much employed by his townsmen and others, but after his return home he always declined to serve them in this capacity, and advised to compromise their lawsuits. Belknap says he was a man of temperance, economy and great industry. His judgment was sound, with strong passions he was yet frank and humane. In politics he was a decided republican, a supporter of the administration of Mr. Jefferson.

He died of the colic Aug., 1799, aged 64 years.

COL. HENRY DEARBORN

Was a descendant of Godfrey Dearborn, who came from England and settled at Exeter, where the colonel was born in March, 1751. He studied medicine with Dr. Hall of Portsmouth, and settled at Nottingham. When the news announcing the action at Lexington arrived he marched for Cambridge the same day.

He was appointed a captain in Stark's regiment, and participated in the battle of Bunker hill. In September he accompanied Arnold in the expedition through the wilderness to Quebec, where he was taken prisoner. The next May he was permitted to return home, *via* Halifax, on his parole. He was exchanged in March following, and was appointed a major in Col. Scammell's regiment, and in May proceeded to Ticonderoga. He fought with his regiment at Saratoga, where he was particularly noticed in Gen. Gates's dispatch for his energy and bravery. He remained with his regiment till the reorganization of the New Hampshire line, Jan. 1st, 1781, when he was made a lieutenant colonel in the first regiment, and on the death of his commander, Col. Scammell, he was promoted to the command of the regiment with the rank of lieutenant colonel commandant and so continued till his *corps* was disbanded about Jan. 1st, 1784. In that year he settled on the Kennebec in Maine. In 1789, he was appointed marshal of that district, and on the accession of Jefferson to the presidency in 1801 he was made secretary of war, which office he held with honor for eight years, when he was made collector of Boston.

In Feb., 1812, he received a commission from the president as major general in the army of the United States. In the spring of the next year he captured York and Fort George, but was recalled and ordered to assume the command of the military district of New York city. When peace was declared he retired to private life. In 1822 he was appointed minister to Portugal, where he remained about two years, when he returned and ever after resided with his son, Gen. Henry Alexander Scammell Dearborn, at Roxbury, where he died in May, 1826.

[The above has been compiled from Allen's *Biographical Dictionary*.]

To this I append the copy of a letter, from which it is inferred he was in company with others engaged in purchasing soldiers' orders or certificates, not always successfully:

"EXETER, July 7, 1783.

"Sir: I have got the thickest of the notes, but there is a considerable number of blanks, some of which I have thought of sending on to you, but I suppose the devl's have given orders for their '82 pay to somebody on the spot, but I wish you to examine the muster, and bring or send on the time William Heath engaged and Ephriam Blood and Jonathan Basson and when

Keys Bradley and John Matthews joined from desertion as I cannot get their notes until I get those returns. Pray get the commanding officer to certify the same. I have hard scrabbling. Orders from all quarters flow in and the prior dates carry the day by which means we have lost several.

"I am your Obedient Servant,
"H. DEARBORN.

"To Lt. Mills or Blake in Camp.

"P. S. Numbers of the men appear here before the committee and swear by all the Gods that they never signed any order."

COL. ALEXANDER SCAMMELL

Was born in that part of the ancient town of Mendon, now Milford, Mass. He graduated at Harvard College in 1769, and was employed a short time in teaching a school at Kingston, Mass., and afterwards at Plymouth, where he was made a member of the Old Colony Club, which about that time held the first celebration of the landing of the Pilgrims at that place.

Early the next year he was at Portsmouth, where, under the auspices of a cousin of the same name in the employment of the government, he entered upon the business of surveying and exploring lands, probably for masts and other timber for the royal navy. This was about 1772.

In an interval of his occupation he kept a school at Berwick, and at one time entered on the study of law with Gen. Sullivan, whom he styles an excellent instructor and worthy patron. He afterwards assisted Capt. Holland in making surveys for his map of New Hampshire. In August, 1772, he was serving on board the sloop Lord Chatham, bound from Pascataqua river to Boston to send reports and plans to England.

Having been a student with Gen. Sullivan, and being an ardent patriot when his instructor was appointed a brigadier in 1775, he did not forget his pupil, but obtained for him the appointment of brigade major. When the New Hampshire regiments were reorganized under the act of congress, Nov., 1776, Maj. Scammell was appointed colonel of Reid's old regiment to be called the Third regiment in the New Hampshire line. The first notice I find of him is the order from the committee of safety, dated Feb. 25, '77, to send forward part or the whole of his regiment to Ticonderoga, as soon as possible. It is not our purpose to follow his career the four years of his service in the other regiments of the New Hampshire line, till by the consolidation of his regiment with the other two, he succeeded Col. Cilley in command of the First regiment, Jan. 1st, 1781.

Previously he held the office of adjutant general of the Continental army, in which he is said to have won the confidence of Gen. Washington to the fullest extent, and the esteem of the officers of his army.

It has been generally supposed that at the time of his death he held no regimental command, but his name is borne on the roll of the First regiment from Jan. 1, 1781, till he was killed Oct. 6th, 1781, as colonel, while Henry Dearborn is ranked as lieutenant colonel. On the memorable siege of Yorktown, Va., Sept. 30th, he was officer of the day, and, while reconnoitering the situation of the enemy, was surprised by a party of their horse, and after being taken prisoner was inhumanly wounded by them. He was conveyed to the city of Williamsburg, where he died October 6th. A monumental tablet was erected to his memory. The above notice is in part compiled from Farmer and Moore's *Collections*, vol. II, p. 166.

In examining some manuscripts relative to military matters at Halifax, N. S., in 1757, I find the name of Alexander Scammell. He was probably an artisan, and perhaps the father of the colonel.

LIEUT. COL. BENJAMIN TITCOMB

Was from Dover. He was one of the most gallant men in the army. He was a captain in Col. Poor's regiment, and a major in Col. Reid's regiment. He was in the battle of Hubbardton, where he was severely wounded. He succeeded Jeremiah Gilman as lieutenant colonel of this regiment, March 24, 1780, and was "deranged"[1] June 1, 1781. He left an honorable

---
[1] Meaning retired.

record in the invalid pension list, viz: "May 14, 1784, Major Benjamin Titcomb of Col. Reid's regiment wounded in three different battles, for half pay from Jan. 1, 1781, to Jan. 1st, 1782, 12 months, £7 10s., £90."

LIEUT. COL. JEREMIAH GILMAN

Was of Epsom. On the reorganization of the regiment, Jan. 1, 1777, he was appointed major, and on the promotion of Cilley to the chief command, Gilman was made lieutenant colonel. He resigned in March, 1780. A search for any further notice of him has proved abortive.

SURGEON NATHANIEL GARDINER

Succeeded Surgeon Hale in June, 1780. He resigned March 1, 1782. A letter from him dated East Hampton, in 1783, may indicate his residence after the war.

MAJOR WILLIAM SCOTT

Was an officer of great energy and bravery, and no doubt his exertions and character did much towards giving efficiency to the regiment under all its difficulties.

He was the son of Alexander Scott, one of the earliest settlers of Peterborough, who went there as early as

1742, but while preparing a residence, he left his wife at Townsend, where William was born May, 1743. His parents were of the Scotch-Irish stock, a hardy, brave people, who contributed not a little to aid the cause of freedom. At the early age of seventeen William Scott enlisted in Goffe's regiment which was raised in New Hampshire in 1760, and aided in the conquest of Canada. At the alarm consequent on Concord fight, he, with many of his townsmen, left their homes for the scene of conflict, and, proceeding on from Concord to Cambridge, he was made a lieutenant in Col. Reid's regiment. At the battle of Bunker hill, early in the action he was wounded, his leg being broken just below the knee; but he continued coolly passing musket balls and handing them to his soldiers. This was necessary, as many of the pieces were only of the smallest calibre, and most of the bullets were too large. When the retreat was ordered he was among the hindmost, and was again wounded in the thigh and body, and, bleeding from four orifices, fainted, and was left on the field. When he came to himself a British soldier was standing over him, with his bayonet, and asking with an oath, if he did not deserve to be killed. "I am in your power do as you please" was the reply. He was taken in charge by a British officer, and remained on the field all night. The next morning he was removed to Boston, and thence to Halifax, where he with many other prisoners were confined. With a gimlet, a bayonet and an old knife, furnished by a friend from the outside, he, with six of his comrades, broke through a door, and, by the further assistance of the same friend, they got on board a small vessel, and reached home in August. He soon rejoined the army near New York, and was one of the garrison of Fort Washington when that was taken; but the night after, tying his sword to his neck and his watch to his hat band, he swam a mile and a half, to near Fort Lee, being the only one that escaped. He was soon promoted to a captaincy in Col. Henry's, a Massachusetts regiment, but preferring a position in a New Hampshire regiment he accepted a captain's commission in this regiment, and enlisted a company mainly from Peterborough, and the towns in that vicinity, under the following order from the committee of safety:

"Feb. 18, 1777.

"Captain William Scott has orders to recruit a company for Col. Stark's regiment."

On the margin of the Ledger, as there is to nearly all the officers at the reorganization, are the words "engaged Nov. 8," and his pay commenced Jan. 1, 1777. He probably marched with his company for Ticonderoga, *via* Number Four, in March. On the promotion of Major Gilman to lieutenant colonel, Sept. 20th, 1777, he was made a major, which office he held for six years. From Aug. 1st, 1780, to July 13th, 1781, he was brigade major. He participated in all the battles and campaigns in which his regiment bore a part, and was renowned everywhere for his bravery as well as his humanity. In an article in Farmer and Moore's *Collection*, vol. II, it is stated, that he "left the regiment and entered the naval service on board the Dean frigate, where he served to the end of the war." This is certainly an error, as the pay rolls, up to Jan. 1, 1783, show he was still holding his former position in the regiment, and the following letter from him written in the autumn to the paymaster, asking him to dispose of his horse which he had left at Albany, shows he must have continued with the regiment till after peace.

"ALBANY, Nov. 13th, 1783.

"Sir: I send my horse and saddle and bridle by Mr. Connely. If you are not supplied he is at your service, at your own price. If you do not need him please to dispose of him, and whatever your trouble may be I will endeavor to reward you. Enclosed is one of [Col.] Beadle's certificates which if you can convert to any use will add to the many obligations I have already experienced. I am sir yours, etc.,

"Wm. Scott.

"P. S. Please present the compliments of this family to John. Mrs. Scott and Mrs. Betsey present their best compliments to you and hope to see you in a few days.

"Lieut. Thomas Blake,
    West Point."

In 1793, he went in the suite of Gen. Lincoln to arrange a treaty with the Six Nations and other Indians, and his portrait is probably among the *corps* of officers and Quakers as figured in Stone's *Life of Brant*, vol. II.

In 1796, he was employed in surveying lands on Black river in northern New York. In this then remote wilderness the party were attacked by the lake fever, and he returned with a part of the sick to Fort Stanwix. Finding it impossible to obtain any person who would go to the relief of the sick who had been left in the wilderness, he determined to go himself, and though very feeble from the disease, and told by the physician he would never return alive, he replied "Some one must go, and my life is no better than theirs." He succeeded in the attempt, but his great exertion in his weak condition cost him his life. He died a few days after his return, at Litchfield, N. Y., Sept. 19, 1796, aged 54 years.

MAJOR JAMES CARR

Was from Somersworth, was a captain in Col. Nathan Hale's regiment. This regiment was broken up at the battle of Hubardston. On the retreat from Ticonderoga, July, 1777, a considerable part of the officers and men were taken prisoners.

He was assigned to this regiment in 1783, and therefore saw no active service in it. He joined the regiment March 1, 1783, and it is likely served till the end of that year.

LIEUT. COL. REID

Was from Londonderry. He was a captain in Col. Stark's regiment formed at Cambridge, April, 1775. Was at Bunker hill, and probably served under him till Jan., 1777. He was lieutenant colonel of the Second regiment, and afterwards its colonel. He took command of this regiment April, 1783, as lieutenant colonel commandant, and served till its dissolution. He was appointed a brigadier of militia 1785, and received the appointment of sheriff of the county of Rockingham, 22 October, 1791. He died in October, 1815, aged 81. His memory is still cherished by the old residents in his native town, as one who in war was always brave and patriotic, and in peace a kind neighbor and valuable citizen.

DOCTOR JOHN HALE

Was in early life settled in Hollis as a physician. In 1755 he was surgeon's mate in Col. Blanchard's New Hampshire regiment in an expedition to Crown point against the French, and in 1758 he was surgeon in Col. Hart's regiment which was in the Crown point expedition of that year.

In 1768 he was representative to the legislature from the associated towns of Hollis and Dunstable, and at the commencement of the revolution he was colonel of a regiment of militia composed of the soldiers from Hollis and the adjoining towns in that vicinity.

He was a member of the convention that sat at Exeter in April, 1775, and assisted in inaugurating the measures to organize the regiments that fought at Bunker hill, and was also in the field a large part of that year.

His sister was the wife of Col. Prescott of Pepperill, *the hero* of Bunker hill, and as their residence was only three miles apart their intercourse was frequent and always friendly. During 1775 and '6 he was much engaged in aiding the cause by raising soldiers as well as assisting in the counsels of the state. On the reorganization of the First regiment he was appointed surgeon, and entered on his duty May 8, 1777. It is supposed that most of the regiment were then at Ticonderoga or on the way there. He was with the regiment all through the campaigns and battles of that year and the next, and in the expedition to the Indian country in 1779, and resigned Jan. 11, 1780. Returning home, his influence was exerted in raising men and means till the end of the war. He was often a member of the legislature, was distinguished as a physician and had a large practice. He died in 1791. The following is the inscription on his tombstone at Hollis:

" Erected to the memory of
Doctor John Hale
who was born Oct. 24, 1731,
and died Oct. 22d, 1791.

" How soon our new born light attains to full ag'd noon,
And that how soon to grey haired night,
We spring, we bud, we blossom and we blast,
Ere we can count our days they fly so fast."

WILLIAM HALE

The son of Doctor Hale, was born at Hollis, July 27, 1762. When less than fifteen years of age he enlisted in this regiment as a private with the understanding that he was to be an aid to his father, probably occupying a position analagous to what is now termed hospital steward. He faithfully served through his term of three years. Returning home, he studied medicine with his father, and succeeded him as a physician.

His practice was extensive in Hollis and the neighboring towns. He was a man of great energy, and enjoyed a very robust constitution. He died in 1852, at the remarkable age of ninety-two. He was the Nestor of the regiment, having no doubt survived all of the some twelve hundred persons whose names are borne on its rolls, and his return from service seventy-two years. Late in life he was instrumental in aiding many of his old comrades in obtaining pensions as his memory was remarkably retentive to the last. He was father of nine children, three of whom are still living.

DOCTOR JONATHAN POOL

Was born at Woburn, Sept. 5, 1758, was the son of Eleazer and Mary Pool. At the age of nineteen he was a student of Doctor Hale's, and by his influence received the appointment of assistant surgeon under him. He entered the service at the same date, and faithfully did his duty for over three years, retiring June 4, 1780. Making Hollis his home he soon commenced the practice of his profession with a prospect of long continued usefulness, but died July 25th, 1797, aged 38.

Among the young men from Hollis who joined this regiment was Ralph Emerson, son of the Rev. Mr. Emerson. He was then but sixteen years of age. He was the associate of young Hale, and they both joined and were discharged on the same days. With every prospect of usefulness he met a sudden death.

The following is the inscription on his grave stone under the representation of a cannon:

"We drop a pace,
  By nature some decay,
  And some the gusts of fortune sweep away."

"Erected to the memory of Lieut. Ralph Emerson, who was instantly killed by the accidental discharge of a cannon while exercising the Mattross, Oct. 4, 1790, in the 30th year of his age."

CAPTAIN MOODY DUSTIN

Was from Litchfield. He was commissioned in the regiment Nov., 1776, as a lieutenant, was promoted to captain, March 5, 1778, and served till the end of December, 1783 — a service of seven years. In the absence of any further details of him the following letter is inserted:

"STONY POINT, Oct. 17, 1783.

"Sir: I would thank you to let me know whether Thomas Hunt has got the months of Feb., March and April for 1783, due to him. Please write the first opportunity.

"As for news I have none, if you have any, pray let me hear from you.

"My compliments to the officers. Tell Maj. Morrell that I want to hear from him as soon as possible.

"Yours to Serve,
"MOODY DUSTIN.

"To Lieut. Blake, paymaster of
The New Hampshire Line,
West Point, N. Y."

Maj. Morrell had been a captain in the First New Hampshire regiment, but was promoted and transferred to the Second New Hampshire regiment. The letter is valuable only as showing that the First regiment was on duty at Stony point. And, also that Lieut. Blake was paymaster then of all that constituted the New Hampshire line.

CAPTAIN ISAAC FRYE

Was from Wilton. He was a quarter master in Col. Reid's regiment, enlisted at Cambridge, April, 1775, was in the battle of Bunker hill, and the regiment remained in service till the following winter.

He was appointed to this regiment, having previously been a captain in the Third regiment. He continued to serve here till Jan., 1784.

CAPTAIN EBENEZER FRYE

Was from Pembroke. He was a first lieutenant in Capt. Daniel Moore's company in Col. Stark's regiment, organized at Cambridge, in April, 1775, and continued in the regiment till about Jan., 1777. His exploits at Trenton are mentioned in the account of that battle. The committee of safety's record is: " gave orders to Capt. Ebenezer Frye to recruit a company for Col. Stark's regiment as soon as possible." In the regimental record it states that he was engaged the November previous, and the pay roll dates his entry Jan. 1, 1777. In a later roll is entered against his name, " cashiered Dec. 6th, 1782." That a veteran officer should receive such a record, after serving more than five and a half years, is to be regretted, perhaps the cause was a trifling one, so no permanent shade rested on his fame.

CAPTAIN DANIEL LIVERMORE

Was born at Watertown, Mass., in 1749. He was descended from a family that were among the earliest settlers of that town. While quite young he came to Concord, N. H., where he served his time as a house carpenter. In June, 1775, he received a commission in Col. Stark's regiment. In November, 1776, he received a commission in the Third regiment in the New Hampshire line, and probably recruited during the winter, and went with his regiment to Ticonderoga in the spring of 1777. Continuing with his regiment in 1779 he was in the expedition to destroy the Indian towns in the western part of the state of New York. During this campaign he kept a journal, which is published in the 6th vol. of the *Collections of the New Hampshire Historical Society.*

When the Third regiment was merged in the First and Second he was transferred to the First, in which he served until December, 1783, when he resigned and returned to Concord, with a brevet appointment of major. He resided in Concord till his death, in 1798, at the age of forty-nine, leaving a reputation as a good and intelligent citizen, and an honest man.

CAPTAIN NATHANIEL HUTCHINGS

Was of Hopkinton. He was a lieutenant and captain in Col. Pierce Long's regiment, which, during the fall of 1776, was stationed near Portsmouth, but in November was ordered to Ticonderoga. It is possible he recruited his company there from the discharged soldiers, as he did not join this regiment till April, 1777. Jan. 1st, 1781, he was retired.

CAPTAIN SIMON SARTWELL

Was of Charlestown. Entered as a lieutenant, Jan. 1, 1777. "September 20, 1777, promoted to a captain lieutenant, with rank and pay of a captain." "Promoted to a captain, March 21, 1780. Discharged May 11, 1781." Such is the record, to which I am unable to add anything.

MAJOR AMOS MORRILL

Was from Epsom. He was first lieutenant of Capt. Dearborn's company in 1775, and was in the battle of Bunker hill. Was engaged as captain in this regiment Nov. 8, 1776, and on pay, Jan. 1, 1777. He was promoted to a major March 24, 1780. He served through the reorganization Jan. 1, 1782, and was acting as major in the summer of 1783.

CAPTAIN AMOS EMERSON

Was from Chester, was lieutenant in Capt. Hutchin's company in Col. Reid's regiment in 1775. He served from Jan. 1, 1777, till March 24, 1780.

MAJOR JASON WAIT

Was from Alstead, of which town he was one of the first settlers in 1763. It is likely he saw service in 1775 and '6. He served as a captain till July 5, 1780, when he was promoted to major, in which position he remained till Jan. 1, 1782, when he retired.

CAPTAIN ISAAC FARWELL

Was from Charlestown. He was first lieutenant in Col. Reid's regiment in 1775, and was at Bunker hill. Served as a captain from Jan. 1, 1777, till the summer of 1783, and perhaps to the end of that year.

CAPTAIN JOSIAH MUNRO

Was appointed a lieutenant Jan. 1, 1777. Was appointed quarter master in 1778, which he held till he was appointed a captain, July 5, 1780. He served till 1783. He was from Amherst.

CAPTAIN DANIEL CLAPP

Was from Hanover. Entered the regiment, Jan. 1, 1777, as a lieutenant, was promoted to a captain, July 5, 1780. He retired, Jan. 1, 1781.

CAPTAIN ASA SENTER

Was from Londonderry, was appointed a lieutenant, to take effect Jan. 1, 1777. He was promoted to a captain, vice Capt. Sartwell, May, 1781, and served till 1782.

CAPTAIN JONATHAN CASS

Was from Exeter. He entered the army as a soldier on the receipt of the news of the British attack on the company at Lexington. He was at Bunker hill, Saratoga, Trenton, Brandywine, Monmouth, Germantown, and under Sullivan in the expedition to the Indian country in 1779.

Most of this time he served as ensign in the Third regiment, then commanded by Col. Scammell, and afterwards as lieutenant and captain in this regiment. He resided in Exeter till 1790, when he took command of a company in the army raised for the defense of the western frontiers. He continued in the army until 1800, retiring with a commission of major. Pleased with the west, Maj. Cass settled on the banks of the Muskingum in Ohio, where he died in August, 1830, aged 77 years, having lived to see his only son, Lewis Cass, one of the most distinguished statesmen in the country.

LIEUT. JONATHAN CILLEY

Was from Nottingham. He was son of Col. Joseph Cilley. He marched from home with the regiment, and was the youth mentioned on a former page as captured at the retreat from Ticonderoga.

ADJUTANT CALEB STARK.

In the year 1758, while at home on a furlough, Capt. John Stark was married to Elizabeth, daughter of Capt. Caleb Page, one of the earliest and most substantial settlers of Dunbarton, N. H. The next spring Capt. Stark again took the field, and during that year he had the satisfaction to know that Quebec, the stronghold of France in America, had fallen into the hands of the English. On December 3d of this year, the subject of this notice was born under the roof of his grandfather at Dunbarton. When Capt. Stark returned from the war and settled at Derryfield, at the request of his grandfather, Caleb was left with them, where he resided till the dawn of the revolution called him to action. In the meantime he had, for that day, acquired a good education.

When the news of the events of the 19th of April reached his residence, young Stark was but sixteen years of age; but the influences exerted by the capture of Canada and the exploits of his father, filled his mind with a desire for a soldier's life, and he made a request to his grandfather to permit him to join his neighbors who were leaving for the seat of war. To this request the grandfather replied, that he was quite too young to become a soldier, and so for a short time the matter rested.

But very early on a morning of June, 1775, he mounted a horse given him by his grandfather, and was soon with a musket by his side on the road towards his father's camp.

On greeting his father at Medford he received the reply that he was yet too young to come there, but he said he had come to try his fortune as a soldier, and only wished an opportunity. He was consigned to the care of Capt. Reid by his father, who commanded a company in Stark's regiment. The next day was fought the battle of Bunker hill, in which our young cadet took a soldier's part. The summer was spent under the tutelage of Capt. Reid, and occasionally with his father at his head quarters, which were at the elegant residence of Col. Royal, which is still standing in Medford. The owner was then within the British lines for safety. The next spring Mr. Stark received a commission as ensign in Col. Reid's company, and proceeded with the regiment to New York and Canada. On the return of the regiment to the vicinity of Ticonderoga, a fatal disease prevailed among the troops, and the adjutant of the First New Hampshire regiment fell a victim. This gave an opportunity for promotion, and Ensign Stark was appointed to fill the position with the rank of lieutenant.

After the retirement of the enemy to winter quarters the regiment marched through New Jersey, and joined Gen. Washington on the western banks of the Delaware, and late in that year Adjutant Stark was with his regiment and an active participator in the brilliant operations at Trenton and Princeton, which closed the campaign for 1776. Soon after these events Adjutant Stark, with his father, returned home, where they found arrangements had been made to reorganize the regiment in which he was to hold the same position under his father's command.

After the battle of Bennington young Stark had permission from his commander to visit his father, and congratulate him on his great success. In the action of October 7th, the adjutant was wounded in the arm, and soon after, as his father had been appointed a brigadier in the Continental line, he selected his son as aid de camp, but the regimental record dates his resignation only from June 1st, 1778.

Lieut. Stark was with his father through the war, and a part of the time acted as brigade major and adjutant general of the northern department.

At the close of the war his attention was turned to mercantile pursuits at Dunbarton.

In 1806 he was engaged in the importing business at Boston. He visited the West Indies in 1798, and England in 1810, where he remained a year transacting business, and traveling at intervals throughout that country. At the commencement of the war of 1812, he engaged in manufacturing at Pembroke, in which business he remained till 1830.

After this time he was engaged in prosecuting a claim for land in Ohio, granted for military services, which, after a long lawsuit, he recovered. He died upon his estate in Tuscarawas county, Ohio, Aug. 26, 1838, aged 78 years and 8 months.

His strongest characteristics were indomitable courage and perseverance, united with coolness and self-possession, which never left him on any occasion. There are still among the business men of Boston some who remember Major Stark, and who speak of him with respect as a merchant, in which capacity they knew him.

The above is mainly compiled from the *Life of Gen. John Stark* by his grandson, where a more extended memoir can be found.

LIEUT. THOMAS BLAKE

Was of Dorchester, Mass. He was the son of Samuel and Patience Blake, and was born Oct. 7, 1752. He was descended from William Blake, who came to Dorchester in 1630, where he was a man of note among the early settlers. Mr. Blake was a carpenter by trade, and early in 1775 was employed in erecting a new building for Dartmouth College at Hanover. When the alarm, consequent on the attack by the British at Lexington and Concord, April 19th, reached there, he, with many of the students and others, left for Concord, or wherever they might be wanted.

After traveling through the woods for one day, they agreed to organize, and chose him as a leader, and when they reached Cambridge, he, with some of the others, joined one of the regiments in which it was supposed he was ensign. During the summer he was with the army on Lake Champlain, and in Canada, till Montreal was captured, when he returned home. In 1776 he was at White Plains, in Col. Baldwin's regiment. In November of that year he received a commission as ensign in Col. Stark's First New Hampshire regiment, which was to be organized under the act of congress, to serve during the war, and was ordered on the recruiting service in the vicinity of Connecticut river, in Cheshire and Grafton counties. This it is supposed was his employment during the winter of 1776 and '7. In May he marched with his men to Charlestown No. 4, and thence to join his regiment at Ticonderoga. He continued with this regiment through all its campaigns and battles till its dissolution, in January, 1784, a period of over seven years. In 1778 he was promoted to a lieutenant, and on the death of Paymaster Kimball, he was appointed to fill his place, and also as regimental clothier. Probably no other man in the regiment was so well fitted to perform these offices as Mr. Blake. He was well versed in accounts, and possessed in a remarkable degree a taste for system and details, and whatever he undertook he did well. This he inherited from his ancestors, who had for generations been remarkable for their skill as surveyors of land, and managers of town affairs. The books of this regiment, so carefully kept by Mr. Blake, and which have been as carefully preserved by his son, bear evidence to his care and fidelity. And the journal of the marches and campaigns of the regiment for about five years are additional evidence of his care and industry.

ter the regiment was disbanded Mr. B. was appointed to settle up with the officers and soldiers, and to effect this he traveled through New Hampshire. Returning to his home he settled in Boston, where he was engaged in manufacturing and selling soap and candles, subsequently under the well known firm of Blake & Jackson, which had a long and respectable career.

As a business man he was noted for his precision and for his scrupulous adherence to truth and honesty, and enjoyed the respect and confidence of a very large acquaintance. His residence was on what was the corner of Washington street and Blake's court, now the eastern part of Union Park street, and his manufactory was between his residence and Harrison Avenue. He died Feb. 16, 1840.

LIEUT. JEREMIAH PRITCHARD

Was the son of Paul Pritchard of Boxford. He was born there in 1754. He removed with his father to New Ipswich in 1772, and they were identified for a long period with the affairs of that town. During the revolution Paul Pritchard was a leading citizen, often a selectman, and represented the town in the legislature.

In 1775 Jeremiah was one of the first to take up arms for his country, he was a soldier in Capt. Towne's company at the battle of Bunker hill, and was afterward, in 1776, near New York, where he was in the battle of White Plains.

In November, 1776, he was commissioned as a lieutenant in this regiment, and probably, like the other officers, spent the winter in enlisting men for the company to which he was assigned, and in the spring went with the regiment to Ticonderoga. In July, 1778, he was appointed adjutant. He was in the various battles, in one of which he was wounded, for which he drew a pension. In 1780 he resigned his office, perhaps on account of his wound; but it is supposed he was afterwards in the service.

After the war he followed the business of a tanner, and was much respected as a citizen. In 1796, a cavalry company was organized there of which he was the first commander. The writer remembers him as a man of fine personal appearance, of great energy, and yet of much dignity and refinement. He had a good education, and often served the town as clerk, and sometimes as its representative. He died in 1813, aged 59.

His brother William enlisted under him, and faithfully served his three years, was in the battles of that period. He returned home, and was a substantial citizen of that town. He succeeded his brother as captain of the company of cavalry, and was killed suddenly in 1835 by being thrown from his chaise, at the age of 75, near the spot where a former captain of that company had been killed by the fall of a tree.

LIEUT. JOSEPH MILLS.

In a letter in the possession of C. H. Bell, Esq., of Exeter, giving an account of his revolutionary services, he stated that he entered as a volunteer in the First New Hampshire regiment in Oct., 1777, and after the surrender of Burgoyne, he was appointed ensign at the special request of Gen. Poor. Being ill from exposure he was sent to New Hampshire on the recruiting service, and remained there till Aug., 1778, by order of Gen. Sullivan. During the winter of 1778 and '9, he was in the same service, and in April, 1779, joined his regiment, and was then for the first time regularly mustered into service. He accompanied the regiment upon the expedition into the Indian country, and served till the end of the war. After this period he settled in Deerfield, and kept a public house there, where he was living in 1792.

By the pay rolls he entered as ensign during 1777, was appointed adjutant May 1, 1780, lieutenant July 5, 1780.

LIEUT. JOSHUA THOMPSON

Was from Londonderry. He was appointed ensign in Capt. Ebenezer Frye's company, Nov. 8th, 1776, but was not put on pay roll till Jan. 1, 1777. He was promoted to a lieutenancy March 5, 1778, and acted as paymaster for a time.

After the war he settled in what is now East Concord. He was a quiet, unobtrusive citizen, of much respectability. In 1824, when Gen. La Fayette visited Concord, he paid Lieut. Thompson the rare compliment of a visit at his house, the lieutenant being unable, on account of age, to join in the ceremonies in honor of the marquis.

LIEUT. JOHN TAGGART.

Was from Peterborough, where he was born. He was of the Scotch-Irish race, by whom the town was settled. Many of them down to the present century preserved the dialect of their fathers, with many other peculiarities. He was a lieutenant in Capt. Isaac Farwell's company at the battle of Bunker hill, where having fought as long as they could fight retreated, and while yet in the midst of danger he stopped his companions, and having refreshed themselves from their canteens, he exclaimed, "Now let us trust in God and take another run."

He did not live to do much service in this regiment, as the roll says, " died July 7th, 1777." It is likely he was killed in the battle which took place that morning on the evacuation of Ticonderoga.

It had entered into the plan of the work to give some account of every officer belonging to the regiment, so far as the facts could be collected. But while materials were abundant for memoirs of the four commanders, and some others, concerning by far the largest number the most thorough researches have yielded only materials for the briefest notices, but we have given all that we could collect.

Having noticed all who attained the rank of captain we shall not attempt even a sketch of the lieutenants or ensigns, as little more than the date of entry and discharge could be added, but will, so far as can be gathered, add their residence. It will be seen that some of them served in the regiment but for a brief period. Lieut. Jonathan Willard was from Charlestown; Lieut. William Bradford, was of Amherst; Lieut. Bezaleel Howe, of Hillsborough; Lieut. Joseph Lawrence, of Walpole; Lieut. William Lee, Lyndeborough; Lieut. Simon Merrill, of Chester.

These are all the names that can be located.

Of the list of officers in this regiment printed in the adjutant general of New Hampshire's report for 1866 (which was probably copied from Farmer & Moore's *Collections*, vol. II), there are eight names that do not appear on any of the pay rolls. It is likely they took commissions conditionally, with beating orders, but could not raise the required number of men, or that there may have been other reasons to prevent their joining the regiment. On the next page we commence to give the names of all the noncommissioned officers and privates who are found on the rolls of the regiment at four different periods. They are arranged in two alphabetical lists with such facts relative to them as could be found.

FIRST NEW HAMPSHIRE REGIMENT. 131

Enlisted Men who served in the First New Hampshire Regiment between Jan., 1777 and Jan., 1782.

Those marked with a * Died of disease or wound, † Killed, D Deserted, M Missing, C Corporal, S Sergeant.

Names.	Where From.	When Entered.	When Discharged.
Stephen Abbot,	Amherst,	Feb. 12, 1777,	June 30, 1781.
John Allen, D	Londonderry,	April 5, 1777,	1780.
Isaac Allds, *	Merrimac,	April 21, 1777,	1778.
David Adams,	Gilsum,	May 18, 1777,	Dec. 31, 1781.
Samuel G. Allen,		March 1, 1779,	Dec. 31, 1781.
Samuel Allen,		Jan. 1, 1777,	Dec. 31, 1781.
John Ash,	Salisbury,	March 8, 1777,	Dec. 31, 1781.
Elijah Averil, C	Amherst,	April 3, 1777,	April 10, 1780.
James Aiken, *	Chester,	April 3, 1777,	July 28, 1777.
Samuel Aiken,	Chester,	April 3, 1777,	April 5, 1780.
Francis Ames, D	Deerfield,	March 21, 1778,	Feb. 5, 1780.
Jonas Adams,	New Ipswich,	Feb. 1, 1777,	Jan. 21, 1780.
David Abraham,	Alstead,	Jan. 1, 1777,	Dec. 31, 1781.
Joel Andrews,	Swanzey,	May 12, 1778,	Dec. 31, 1780.
Aaron Adams,		May 12, 1778,	Dec. 31, 1781.
Isaac Adams,	Hampton,	March 10, 1778,	July 10, 1781.
Elisha Adams, D	Charlestown,	April 10, 1777,	Jan. 10, 1779.
Samuel Adam,	Packersfield,	May 5, 1781,	1781.
John Adams,		Feb. 14, 1781,	Dec. 31, 1781.
Ebenezer Allen,		March 1, 1780,	Dec. 31, 1783.
Timothy Abbot,	Wilton,	Feb. 27, 1781,	Dec. 31, 1781.

Enlisted Men who served in the First New Hampshire Regiment — continued.

NAMES.	WHERE FROM.	WHEN ENTERED.	WHEN DISCHARGED.
Nathan Aldrich,			
Daniel Ashley, *	Walpole,	Feb. 9, 1781,	Aug. 1, 1781.
Levi Adams, S.	New Ipswich,	Feb. 7, 1777,	Feb., 1780.
Nathaniel Andrews, D		May, 1777,	April 30, 1779.
Bezia Beede,		March 15, 1780,	
Jonathan Black,	Londonderry,	Feb. 12, 1781,	Dec. 31, 1781.
Charles Branscomb,	Hampton,	April 13, 1781,	Dec. 31, 1781.
William Brown,	Henniker,	July 13, 1781,	Dec. 31, 1781.
Daniel Barker,	Duxbury, Mile Slip,	Feb. 7, 1781,	Dec. 31, 1781.
Hart Balch,	Dublin,	April 24, 1781,	Dec. 31, 1781.
Nathaniel Barrett,	Mason,	Feb. 27, 1781,	Dec. 31, 1781.
Asa Blood,			
Josiah Burton,		Dec. 10, 1776,	Dec. 31, 1781.
Joel Baker,	New Ipswich,	March 6, 1781,	Dec. 31, 1781.
Keys Bradley,	Concord,	1781,	Dec. 31, 1781.
Ephraim Blood,	Dunstable,	Feb. 1, 1781,	Dec. 31, 1781.
Amunia Bohonnon,	Salisbury,	March 13, 1781,	Dec. 31, 1781.
Nathaniel Batchelder,	Lyndeboro,	March 20, 1777,	March, 1780.
John Batler, M	Dunstable,	April 23, 1777,	
Charles Bowles,		Feb. 2, 1778,	Dec. 5, 1782.
John Berry, †	Chester,	April 1, 1777,	Oct. 7, 1777.
James Boyes,	Londonderry,	Nov. 14, 1776,	Nov. 18, 1779.

FIRST NEW HAMPSHIRE REGIMENT. 133

Name	Town	Enlisted	Discharged
David Bryant,	Weare,	Nov. 12, 1776,	Dec., 1781.
James Brown,	Windham,	April 1, 1777,	Dec., 1780.
Joseph Bark,		Feb. 9, 1777,	Dec., 1781.
Christopher Billings, D.		Jan. 15, 1777,	Dec., 1777.
Jacob Bonney,*		May 20, 1777,	July, 1778.
William Batchelder,	Surry,	Jan. 10, 1777,	Jan. 1, 1780.
James Bowles,	Boscawen,	April 14, 1777,	Dec., 1780.
John Brown, D.	New London,	April, 1779,	1780.
Jonathan Burrows, ‡	Godstown,	Jan. 1, 1777,	Jan. 3, 1780.
Asa Boutwell,	Chester,	1777,	1780.
John Baldwin, D	Walpole,	Dec. 21, 1777,	1780.
Jethro Barber,	Kingston,	March 22, 1781,	Dec., 1781.
Peter Bullard,	New Ipswich,	Feb. 16, 1781,	Dec., 1781.
Amos Baker,	New Ipswich,	Feb. 27, 1781,	Dec., 1781.
John Barlow,		Oct. 6, 1781,	Dec., 1781.
John Barrot,		Oct. 15, 1781,	Dec., 1781.
Samuel Bates,	Claremont,	May 1, 1777,	May 1, 1780.
John Bartlet, †		May 5, 1777,	Sept., 1777.
John Brown,		March 10, 1777,	Aug., 1778.
Moses Brown, † *	Mile Slip,	May 1, 1777,	Oct. 7, 1777.
Benjamin Bevens,*		Feb. 1, 1777,	June 1, 1779.
Nathaniel Bartlet,		May 1, 1777,	April 30, 1780.
Thomas Bates, D.	Poplin,	March 25, 1778,	Oct. 1779.
Samuel Boyd,	Hollis,	March 1, 1778,	Dec., 1781.
Joshua Blodgett,	Derryfield,	March 4, 1777,	March 4, 1780.
James Beverly,	Nottingham,	Jan. 4, 1777,	Dec., 1781.

Enlisted Men who served in the First New Hampshire Regiment — continued.

Names.	Where From.	When Entered.	When Discharged.
Benjamin Brown,	Chichester,	March 1, 1779,	Dec., 1781.
Benjamin Berry,	Chichester,	April 27, 1779,	Dec., 1781.
Cæsar Burns,		Jan., 1777,	Dec., 1781.
Peter Brewer, (Negro) *	New Boston,	March 18, 1777,	Oct. 7, 1777.
Benjamin Butler,	Nottingham,	March 5, 1777,	Mar. 20, 1780.
Josiah Burton,		Jan. 1, 1777,	Dec., 1781.
William Brown,	Amherst,	Jan. 1, 1777,	Dec., 1781.
John Bishop,		Jan. 1, 1777,	Dec., 1780.
Enos Bishop, *	Boscawen,	Jan. 1, 1777,	Aug. 8, 1778.
Nathaniel Bates, * †	Dublin,	Jan. 10, 1777,	Sept. 19, 1777.
Alpheus Butler,		Jan. 1, 1778,	Dec., 1781.
Ripley Bingham, S	Alstead,	Jan. 1, 1779,	Nov. 18, 1779.
Abner Bingham,	Lemster,	March, 1777,	Dec., 1781.
Benjamin Barnet,	Haverhill,	Feb. 17, 1777,	Jan. 25, 1780.
Nathaniel Bagbee,		April 22, 1777,	April 23, 1780.
Isaac Boynton,	Hollis,	April 10, 1777,	April 10, 1780.
Daniel Blood, *	Hollis,	April 10, 1777,	Nov. 28, 1778.
Robert Burts,	Nottingham West,	April 28, 1777,	July 8, 1780.
Thomas Baxter, *		April 28, 1777,	Dec. 31, 1777.
Sanders Bradbury, *		April 1, 1777,	Nov. 15, 1779.
Peter Bryer, *	Epping,	April 28, 1777,	April 1, 1778.
Ebenezer Berry,	Chester,	April 1, 1777,	March 20, 1780.

FIRST NEW HAMPSHIRE REGIMENT. 135

Noah Baswell,	....	....	Jan. 21, 1780.
Scipio Brown, D.,	....	March 10, 1777,	Nov. 10, 1777.
Simeon Butterfield,	Dunstable,	March 1, 1777,	Jan. 25, 1780.
Samuel Barrons,	Lyndeboro,	May 1, 1778,	May 26, 1780.
Moses Chase,	....	May 1, 1777,	April 30, 1780.
Jonathan Cochran, *	Amherst,	April 5, 1777,	March 24, 1778.
John Clark,	Claremont,	May 1, 1777,	April 30, 1780.
James Campbell,	Lyndeboro,	March 4, 1779,	Oct., 1780.
John Combs,	Merrimac,	April 21, 1777,	April 22, 1780.
John Cowdrey,	Merrimac,	April 21, 1777,	Dec., 1780.
Benjamin Cotton,	....	....	....
Solomon Chapman,	Concord,	Feb. 1, 1777,	Dec., 1781.
Robert Crawford, *	....	Jan. 1, 1777,	Sept. 22, 1778.
Theophilus Cass, S.,	Epsom,	Jan. 1, 1777,	Dec., 1781.
Robert Cunningham,	Amherst,	April, 1777,	Dec., 1781.
William Cook, D.,	....	March 7, 1777,	1781.
John Caldwell, *	....	April, 1779,	Dec., 1781.
Curtiss Cady,	....	Feb., 1777,	April 1, 1778.
Edward Carter,	Hollis,	Feb. 1, 1777,	Jan. 21, 1780.
William Connell,	Hollis,	Feb. 1, 1777,	Jan. 21, 1780.
Jonathan Conant,	....	April 22, 1777,	April 20, 1780.
Thomas Clark,	....	April 14, 1777,	April 14, 1778.
Jonathan Currier,	....	April 24, 1777,	July 28, 1777.
Josiah Clark, *	Nottingham,	May 9, 1779,	Nov. 20, 1781.
Thomas Colburn,	Litchfield,	Jan., 1777,	Jan., 1780.
Bishop Coster,	Londonderry,	April 9, 1777,	April 10, 1780.

Enlisted Men who served in the First New Hampshire Regiment — continued.

NAMES.	WHERE FROM.	WHEN ENTERED.	WHEN DISCHARGED.
Zebulon Colbie, *	Chichester,	Jan. 10, 1777,	Oct. 7, 1779.
James Campbell,	Londonderry,	Jan., 1777,	May, 1780.
Bunker Clark,	Packersfield,	Feb. 3, 1777,	Dec., 1781.
Benjamin Crichet,		Feb., 1777,	Sept., 1777.
Thomas Church,	} Unknown.		
James Cochrane,			
John Cross, C	Swanzey,	Jan. 1, 1778,	Dec. 31, 1781.
John Clark,	Hempstead,	Feb. 3, 1777,	Dec. 31, 1781.
Samuel Caldwell, S	Weare,	July 3, 1777,	July 2, 1780.
Enos Challis, C	Hawke,	May 7, 1777,	Dec. 31, 1780.
Daniel Creesy,	Hopkinton,	April 10, 1777,	April 10, 1779.
Samuel Cammitt,	Kingston,	March 1, 1777,	Feb. 20, 1780.
Joshua Church,	Surry,	March 18, 1777,	April 30, 1780.
Moses Colby,	Hopkinton,	April 4, 1777,	April 4, 1780.
Thomas Cammet,	Kingston,	March 18, 1777,	March 18, 1780.
Benjamin Collins, *	Dunbarton,	Jan. 18, 1778,	July 22, 1778.
John Cooper,	Plastow,	April 27, 1778,	Dec. 31, 1781.
Ephraim Cross, D	Hopkinton,	April 16, 1777,	1780.
John Chadwick, S	Hopkinton,	April 6, 1777,	April 5, 1780.
John T. Conner,	Hopkinton,	April 8, 1777,	April 5, 1780.
Robert Cunningham,	Amherst,	April 18, 1777,	Nov. 5, 1778.
Timothy Curtiss,		Jan. 1, 1777,	Sept. 18, 1778.

FIRST NEW HAMPSHIRE REGIMENT. 137

Name		Date	Date
Isaac Calcof,	Taken prisoner,	April 18, 1777,	July 7, 1778.
Benjamin Critcher,		April 20, 1780,	Dec. 31, 1781.
Eliphlet Caswell, D		July 29, 1780,	June 4, 1781.
Salem Colby,		March 1, 1780,	Dec. 31, 1781.
Daniel Clough,		Jan. 1, 1781,	Dec. 31, 1781.
Thomas Cross,		Served 20 days,	1780.
Moses Chase,		Served 20 days,	1780.
Gilbert Caswell, S	Salisbury,		
Ebenezer Collins, S		July 8, 1777,	Dec., 1781.
Isaac Clements, S*	Newport,	April 6, 1777,	Oct., 1777.
Edmund Colby,	Hopkinton,	Jan. 1, 1781,	Dec. 31, 1780.
Daniel Colby,	Canterbury,	March 23, 1781,	Oct., 1781.
Stephen Colby, +	Canterbury,	March 23, 1781,	Dec. 31, 1781.
Eliphlet Cole,	Warner,	Feb. 21, 1781,	Nov. 2, 1781.
Benjamin Cressy,		April,	Dec., 1781.
Alva Currier,	Hopkinton,	April 6, 1781,	March 17, 1782.
James Chamberlin,	Hopkinton,	April 5, 1781,	Dec., 1781.
Francis Connor,	Dublin,	April 24, 1781,	Dec., 1781.
Moses Cutter,	New London,	April 23, 1781,	Dec., 1781.
Abiel Chandler,		March 16, 1781,	Dec., 1781.
Thomas Capron, D	Jaffrey,	March 20, 1781,	Dec., 1781.
John Colburn,	Candia,	April 18, 1778,	June, 1778.
Hezakiah Clark, *		April 20, 1777,	April, 1780.
Cyprl Child, * S		Jan. 1, 1777,	Dec., 1781.
Jonas Cutting, * C	Bedford,	March 1, 1777,	1778.
Rowlins Coburn, S*	New Ipswich,	Jan. 1, 1777,	1780.

18

Enlisted Men who served in the First New Hampshire Regiment — continued.

Names.	Where From.	When Entered.	When Discharged.
Philemon Ducit,	Temple,	......, ...,	1781.
John Dole,	Jaffray,	Jan., 1777,	May, 1780.
Thomas Davis,	Merrimac,	May, 1777,	April, 1780.
William Durrah, S	Windham,	April, 1777,	1780.
Joshua Danford,	New Andover,	Jan., 1777,	Dec., 1771.
Benjamin Dow,	Northwood,	Jan., 1777,	Dec., 1781.
James Dickey,	Merrimac,	March, 1777,	Dec., 1781.
John Door,*	....	Feb., 1777,	Oct. 7, 1777.
John Davis,*	Madbury,	Jan., 1777,	April 15, 1778.
John Dwire,*	Allenstown,	Jan., 1777,	July, 7, 1777.
Nathaniel Dickey,	Epsom,	April, 1779,	Dec., 1781.
Richard Brought,	....	April, 1779,	Dec., 1781.
Ezekiel Davis,*	Amherst,	Jan., 1777,	June 16, 1779.
Joseph Davis,*	Amherst,	Jan., 1777,	Aug. 13, 1779.
Charles Dougherty,	....	Jan., 1777,	Dec., 1781.
Lemuel Dean,	....	March, 1777,	March, 1780.
Thomas Duncan,*	....	May, 1777,	Nov., 1778.
Nathan Davis,	....	March, 1778,	Feb., 1781.
Reuben Dunnell,	Lyndeboro,	March, 1777,	March, 1780.
Jacob Payne, S	....	Jan., 1777,	May, 1781.
Samuel Dolton,	Chester,	Feb., 1777,	Jan., 1780.
David Dickey,	....	April, 1777,	April, 1780.

FIRST NEW HAMPSHIRE REGIMENT.

Name	Town		
John Douglass, D	Hawke,		1780.
Samuel Danford,	Canterbury,	Jan. 1, 1778,	Dec., 1781.
William Dickey,	Francestown,	April, 1778,	April, 1780.
Stephen Dustin,		April, 1777,	May, 1782.
John Dornan,	Dunbarton,	April, 1778,	Dec., 1781.
James Doud,	Newport,	Jan., 1778,	Dec., 1781.
Samuel Davis,	Goffestown,	Jan., 1777,	Dec., 1781.
Zephaniah Downs,		July, 1779,	Dec., 1781.
Benjamin Bockum,		Feb., 1780,	Dec., 1781.
Nicholas Dodge,	Londonderry,	Jan., 1780,	Dec., 1781.
Benjamin Pole,		March, 1781,	Dec., 1781.
Thomas Dodge,	Jaffray,	April, 1781,	May, 1780.
Benj Dickey,*		May 1777,	Sept. 19, 1777.
Ralph Ellingwood,		March 1777,	Feb. 14, 1781.
Samuel Eyers,*	Dunstable,	April 3, 1778,	Feb. 17, 1780.
John Elliot,*	Madbury,	March 18, 1778,	May 20, 1778.
Jonathan Eastman,*	Walpole,	Jan. 1, 1777,	May 11, 1778.
John Elliot,*		Feb. 21, 1777,	Oct. 7, 1777.
Ralph Emerson,	Hollis,	Jan. 4, 1777,	April 10, 1780.
Edward Evans,	Boscawin,	April 10, 1777,	Dec., 1781.
Samuel Eyers,	Londonderry,	Feb. 7, 1777,	April 30, 1780.
Jacob Eastman,		April 28, 1777,	Dec., 1781.
Ira Evans, D		May 1, 1779,	May 8, 1779.
Joseph Eastman,*	Hopkinton,	Jan. 1, 1777,	Oct. 30, 1777.
John Eastman, Sen.*	Hopkinton,	April 10, 1777,	July 8, 1777.
John Eastman, Jr.,	Hopkinton,	April 10, 1777,	
		May 6, 1778,	

Enlisted Men who served in the First New Hampshire Regiment — continued.

Names.	Where From.	When Entered.	When Discharged.
Noah Emery,	Pembroke,	April 10, 1777,	Jan. 1, 1778.
Daniel Emery,			
Henry Eastman,	Henska,	July 13, 1781,	Dec., 1781.
Josiah Eastman,	London,	April 26, 1781,	1781.
Samuel Eastman,		Feb. 24, 1778,	Aug. 24, 1778.
Joseph Ellison,	London,	April 26, 1781,	Dec., 1781.
John Eaton,	Hopkinton,	April 5, 1781,	Dec., 1781.
Phillip Flanders,	Boscawen,	Jan. 1, 1777,	June 1, 1782.
Daniel Fuller, D		March 1, 1777,	April, 1779.
Antonia Foster, *		Feb. 17, 1777,	July 7, 1777.
Thomas Fuller,	Landown,	April 3, 1777,	Dec., 1781.
Samuel Fugard,	Bedford,	Jan. 1, 1777,	Nov. 3, 1782.
Robert Forrest,	London,	March 1778,	Feb. 26, 1781.
Moses Farnsworth,	Alstead,	Feb. 1, 1777,	Feb. 1, 1780.
Elpir Frost, D	Negro,	Jan. 18, 1778,	Sept. 25, 1778.
Ephraim Foster, S	New Ipswich,	Feb. 1, 1777,	July 6, 1778.
John Flanders,	Weare,	Feb. 10, 1777,	Jan. 25, 1780.
Elijah Fairfield,	Hawke,	April 17, 1777,	April 20, 1780.
Jacob Flanders,	Weare,	Feb. 20, 1777,	Dec., 1781.
Wm. Frankford, *	Swanzey,	Jan. 9, 1778,	April 17, 1779.
John S. Farnham, C	Hopkinton,	May 5, 1779,	Dec., 1781.
Ebenezer Forgtae, *		Feb. 1 1777,	Nov. 14, 1777.

Joshua Fall,		March 29, 1780,	Dec. 1781.
Phineas Fletcher,*		March 23, 1781,	Dec. 1, 1781.
Timo Farnham,	Canterbury,	April 5, 1781,	
Gideon Fletcher,	Hopkinton,	March 17, 1781,	Dec. 1781.
Nathan Foster,	Cockermouth,	March 10, 1781,	Dec. 1781.
William Fuzier, D		May 10, 1781,	Sept. 30, 1777.
Thomas George,		Jan. 1, 1777,	Jan. 25, 1780.
Isaac George,	Nottingham,	March 1, 1777,	Jan. 25, 1780.
Benjamin George,	Derryfield,	March 1, 1777,	Jan. 25, 1780.
Nathaniel Graham,	Derryfield,	Feb. 19, 1778,	Dec. 1781.
Joseph Grant,	Deering,	March 5, 1778,	Dec. 14, 1780.
Nehemiah Gold,*	Stratham,	April 29, 1777,	Aug. 10, 1778.
Moses Gold,*	Westmoreland,	April 29, 1777,	Jan. 10, 1778.
Isaac Gibbs,		March 10, 1777,	March 20, 1780.
Joshua Gibbs,	Hinsdale,	Feb. 7, 1777,	March 20, 1780.
Simeon Gould,		March 10, 1777,	Jan. 21, 1780.
David Gibbs,	Lyme,	March 10, 1777,	March 20, 1780.
Asa Goodale,*		Feb. 17, 1777,	July 7, 1777.
Duncan Grant,	Hampstead,	April 4, 1777,	Dec. 31, 1780.
Thomas Gouth,	Lyndeboro,	March 23, 1777,	March 20, 1780.
George Gouth,	Bedford,	Jan. 1, 1777,	Nov. 18, 1779.
William Goffe,*	Bedford,	April 12, 1777,	Sept. 19, 1777.
Nathaniel Glines,	Canterbury,	June 9, 1777,	Dec. 1781.
James Gilmore,	Windham,	April 25, 1777,	April 5, 1780.
Thomas Gilmore,	Newport,	Jan. 1, 1777,	Nov. 18, 1779.
Silas Gill, (wounded)	New Ipswich,	Feb. 1, 1777,	Dec. 1779.

142 HISTORY OF THE

Enlisted Men who served in the First New Hampshire Regiment — continued.

Names.	Where From.	When Entered.	When Discharged.
Matthew Grear,	Lempster,	March 16, 1778,	Dec., 1781.
John Grout,		May 1, 1778,	Dec., 1781.
Charles Greenfield.	Hawke,	April 12, 1777,	April 22, 1780.
Thomas George.	Dunbarton,	April 17, 1779,	April 20, 1780.
Anthony Gilman,	Surry.	July 1, 1777,	Taken prisoner.
Winsor Gleason,			
John Gaffett,		Jan. 24, 1780,	Dec., 1781.
Daniel Gage, S.	Pelham,	Dec. 29, 1779,	Dec., 1781.
Joseph Gilman.		Jan. 11, 1780,	Dec., 1781.
John Grow.		March 1, 1780,	Dec., 1781.
William Glines.	Canterbury,	Feb. 17, 1781,	Dec., 1781.
John Gault,	Bedford,	March 12, 1781,	Dec., 1781.
Jona Griffin,	Derryfield,	March 8, 1781,	Dec., 1781.
Benjamin W. Grace.	Hollis,	May 28, 1781,	Dec., 1781.
John Greeley,	Pelham,	March 9, 1781,	Dec., 1781.
Daniel Gould,	Fitzwilliam,	Feb. 22, 1781,	Dec., 1781.
John Ablot Goss,	Amherst.	March 15, 1781,	Dec., 1781.
William Gregory,	Rye.	April 7, 1781,	Dec., 1781.
Jona Griffin,*	Deerfield,	April 5, 1781,	Oct. 1, 1781.
Joseph Grant,	Deerfield,	April 13, 1781,	Dec., 1781.
William Hodgkins,		April 6, 1777,	April 5, 1780.
Enoch Hoit.	Hopkinton,	July 3, 1777,	July 2, 1780.

FIRST NEW HAMPSHIRE REGIMENT. 143

Thomas Harvey,	Nottingham,	June 1, 1779,	Dec., 1781.
Joseph Henderson,	Peterborough,	Jan. 1, 1777,	Jan. 1, 1778.
John P. Hilton,	Nottingham,	Jan. 1, 1777,	Feb. 1, 1779.
Sylvanus Hastings,		Jan. 1, 1778,	Dec., 1779.
William Hewett, C.	New Ipswich,	Feb. 1, 1778,	Dec., 1781.
Matthew Holcomb, D.	Boscawin,	Jan. 1, 1777,	July 9, 1777.
Joseph Hadley, D.	Goffstown,	Jan. 1, 1777,	Sept. 2, 1779.
Benjamin Hudson, *	Walpole,	June 9, 1777,	
Robert Holland,	Candia,	Feb. 2, 1778,	Aug. 5, 1781.
David Hill, D.	Candia,	Feb. 2, 1777,	Oct. 1, 1778.
Benoni Hill,		Jan. 25, 1780,	Dec., 1781.
Samuel Harper, D.	Ackworth,	Jan. 1, 1777,	Aug. 8, 1778.
Thomas Harper, D.	Ackworth,	Jan. 1, 1777,	Aug. 8, 1778.
John Humble,	Portsmouth,	Feb. 25, 1780,	Dec., 1781.
Thomas Hunt,	Richmond,	Feb. 1, 1778,	Dec., 1781.
David Howe, C.		Jan. 1, 1780,	Dec., 1781.
Cato Hale,			
Israel Hale,	Lyndborough,	Feb. 26, 1781,	Oct., 1781.
Ephraim Hildreth,	Hopkinton,	April 5, 1781,	Dec., 1781.
Israel Howes, C.	Wilton,	Feb. 27, 1781,	Dec., 1781.
Daniel Holt,	Wilton,	Jan. 27, 1781,	Dec., 1781.
Daniel Harper,	Jaffrey,	March 19, 1781,	Dec., 1781.
Moses Heath,	Salem,	April 6, 1781,	Dec., 1781.
Joseph B. Hoit,	Kinsington,	March 21, 1781,	Dec., 1781.
Joseph Homan,	Kingston,	April 7, 1781,	Dec., 1781.
Aaron Hayes,		March 26, 1781,	Dec., 1781.

Enlisted Men who served in the First New Hampshire Regiment — continued.

Names.	Where From.	When Entered.	When Discharged.
Elnır Hoey,	Epping,	March 3, 1781,	Dec., 1781.
Joseph Hodgman,	Mason,	May 6, 1781,	Dec., 1781.
George Hogg,			
Simeon Hutchins,			March 1, 1782.
John Harper, D	Ackworth,	April 2, 1777,	
Joel Holt,	Wilton,	Jan. 23, 1777,	Dec., 1781.
John Hillsgrove, D	Temple,	Feb. 27, 1781,	July, 1781.
Joseph Hills,	Merrimack,	Jan. 1, 1777,	May 4, 1780.
Ebenezer Hills,	Merrimack,	April 1, 1777,	April 20, 1780.
Jere Hazilton.*		April 21, 1777,	May 12, 1778.
Joseph Hazleton,	Derryfield,	Jan. 1, 1777,	Jan., 1780.
Jonathan Hazelton,	Gillmantown,	Feb. 12, 1777,	Dec., 1781.
Elijah Hutcherson, D	London,	Jan. 1, 1777,	Nov., 1781.
Levi Hutcherson,	North Ward,	April 20, 1778,	Dec., 1781.
Henry Harris,		April 9, 1777,	April 10, 1780.
Barabas Hickey,*	Charlestown,	Jan. 1, 1777,	April 14, 1778.
Solomon Harris,		March 22, 1778,	Dec., 1781.
Samuel Hill,	Hollis,	April 10, 1777,	April, 1780.
Jonas Hubbart,		March 22, 1777,	March 25, 1780.
Samuel Hews,		April 18, 1777,	April 20, 1780.
John Hazelton,	Cockamouth,	Feb. 1, 1777,	Feb. 1, 1780.
Roswell Howard,		April 18, 1777,	June 12, 1778.

FIRST NEW HAMPSHIRE REGIMENT. 145

William Hale,	Hollis,	April 10, 1777,	April 10, 1778.
James Hardy,		Feb. 13, 1777,	July 1, 1778.
John Hutchinson,*		Jan. 26, 1777,	June 22, 1778.
Samuel Hoit,	Chester,	March 14, 1777,	Dec. 1781.
Jesse Heath,		April 25, 1777,	April 30, 1780.
Nathaniel Hardy,*	Nottingham, West,	May 1, 1777,	March 5, 1781.
Calvin Honey,*		Dec. 3, 1779,	Dec. 15, 1781.
James Herod,	Dunstable,	April 17, 1777,	Dec. 1, 1777.
David Hunt,		Jan. 1, 1778,	Dec. 1781.
Zacheus Hunt,	Poplin,	Feb. 1, 1778,	Dec. 1781.
Jeremiah Hobnan,		Nov. 15, 1776,	Nov. 18, 1799.
Robert Hodgart,	Londonderry,	March 12, 1777,	April 1, 1786.
Timothy Herrington,	Londonderry,	Jan. 1, 1777,	Nov. 18, 1799.
Levi Hoit,*		May 15, 1777,	Dec. 1781.
Timothy Hutchinson,	Deerfield,	April 1, 1777,	Oct. 7, 1777.
John Hall,	Londonderry,	March 12, 1778,	Dec. 1781.
John Head,	London,	Jan. 1, 1777,	Dec. 1781.
Thomas Haines,	Peterborough,	April 15, 1777,	April 26, 1781.
James Hawley,	New Ipswich,	March 1, 1777,	Dec. 1781.
Nathaniel Hays, C	Charlestown,	Feb. 1, 1777,	Jan. 21, 1781.
Paye Harriman,		May 19, 1777,	May 20, 1780.
Moses Hutchins,		Jan. 1, 1777,	Dec. 1781.
Asa Holt, D	Dunbarton,	Feb. 13, 1777,	Aug. 8, 1778.
Peter Hersey,*		April 8, 1777,	Jan. 20, 1778.
Jonathan Judkins,*	Barnstead,	June 21, 1777,	March 4, 1778.
John Jenness,	Epsom,	April 20, 1779,	Dec. 1781.

19

Enlisted Men who served in the First New Hampshire Regiment — continued.

Names.	Where From.	When Entered.	When Discharged.
Francis Joiner,	Walpole,	Jan. 1, 1777,	Nov. 18, 1779.
David Johnson, S		April 16, 1777,	Dec., 1781.
Stephen Jennens, C	New Grantham,	May 12, 1777,	May 20, 1780.
Ephraim Jennens, *	New Grantham,	May 12, 1777,	Nov. 22, 1777.
Israel Ingalls,		Jan. 27, 1777,	Jan. 21, 1780.
Joel Judkins, †		Feb. 27, 1777,	Oct. 7, 1771.
Peter Jenkins,	Londonderry,	April 17, 1777,	June 20, 1780.
John Joiner, S	Charlestown,	Jan. 1, 1777,	Nov. 18, 1779.
Jona Judkins,	Hopkinton,	April 10, 1777,	April 10, 1780.
John Jorden, D	New Boston,	March 1, 1777,	Jan. 1, 1780.
Thomas Johnson,	Walpole,	Jan. 1, 1777,	Dec., 1781.
Asa Jackson,	Washington,	April 18, 1781,	Dec., 1781.
Philip Judkins, D		Jan. 1, 1777,	Aug. 8, 1778.
Thomas Kimball,		June 3, 1778,	Dec., 1781.
William Kemp, *	Goffertown,	Jan. 4, 1777,	Sept. 6, 1777.
Daniel Kidder,	Amherst,	April 22, 1777,	July 1, 1781.
Simon Knowles,		Jan. 1, 1777,	Dec., 1781.
Jesse Knott, *		Jan. 1, 1777,	July 18, 1778.
Alpheus Kingsley,		Jan. 1, 1777,	July, 1781.
George Knox,	Candia,	May 1, 1778,	May 1, 1781.
John Kent,		Feb. 4, 1778,	Dec., 1781.
Amos Kenney, †	Nottingham West,	April 3, 1777,	Oct. 7, 1777.

FIRST NEW HAMPSHIRE REGIMENT. 147

Jona Knock,	....	March 10, 1777,	March 20, 1780.
Samuel Knox, *	....	Feb. 1, 1777,	Aug. 4, 1778.
Giles Kelsey,	Newport,	April 18, 1777,	April 18, 1780.
Jonathan Kelley,	Epping,	Jan. 1, 1777,	Dec. 1781.
Reuben Kidder,	Goffestown,	Feb. 27, 1781,	Jan. 1, 1781.
William Kimball,	Moultonborough,	June 13, 1781,	Dec., 1781.
Samuel Lee, *	Peterborough,	Jan. 1, 1777,	March 28, 1778.
Orson Lock, †	Kennington,	April 14, 1777,	Sept. 19, 1777.
Moses Lock,	Epsom,	Jan. 19, 1777,	Dec. 1781.
Samuel Lock,	Epsom,	Feb. 1, 1777,	Dec. 1781.
John Loverin,	....	April 15, 1779,	Dec. 1781.
John Lapish,	....	Jan. 1, 1777,	Dec. 1781.
Abel Lovejoy,	....	Feb., 1777,	Jan. 1780.
Asa Lovejoy, †	....	Feb., 1777,	Sept. 19, 1777.
William Lund,	Dunstable,	Feb. 1, 1777,	July 1777.
Icabod Lovell, *	Dunstable,	April 17, 1777,	Oct. 14, 1781.
William Lewey,	Concord,	April 1, 1777,	March, 1780.
James Lamb,	Hopkinton,	March 10, 1777,	Dec. 1781.
William Layton, *	Lempster,	May 3, 1777,	Aug. 4, 1778.
Samuel Lanakee, *	....	Jan. 1, 1777,	Oct. 7, 1777.
Charles Lines,	....	Jan. 14, 1777,	Dec. 1779.
Samuel Liscomb,	Surry,	May 8, 1777,	Dec. 1781.
Stephen Lord,	....	Jan. 1, 1777,	Dec. 1781.
John Larrabee,	Hampton Falls,	Jan. 1, 1777,	Dec. 1780.
Samuel Lock,	Ireland,	April 17, 1779,	Dec. 1780.
Michael Logus, D	....	June, 1779,	Aug. 21, 1781.

148   HISTORY OF THE

Enlisted Men who served in the First New Hampshire Regiment — continued.

NAMES.	WHERE FROM.	WHEN ENTERED.	WHEN DISCHARGED.
William Lang,	Litchfield,	Feb. 18, 1777,	May, 1781.
John Lary, D.		Jan. 4, 1777,	Nov. 1777.
Timothy Lock,		1780,	Dec., 1781.
Noah Levins,	Warner,	Jan. 1, 1781,	March, 1780.
Isaac Lowell,		May, 1781,	Dec., 1781.
William Lowell,		May, 1781,	Dec., 1781.
John Loving,	Pelham,	April, 1781,	Dec., 1781.
Andrew Law,	Temple,	March 16, 1781,	Dec., 1781.
Levi Lufkin,	Salisbury,	April 9, 1781,	Dec., 1781.
William Lakin,		April 4, 1780,	Dec., 1781.
John Millett,*	Temple,	Feb. 15, 1777,	Dec., 1779.
Philip Mahene,*		Jan. 1, 1777,	June 5, 1778.
Thomas McNeale,	New Boston,	April 5, 1777,	Dec., 1781.
William Munn,	Washington,	April 1, 1777,	March 20, 1780.
Nathan Munn,	Washington,	April 1, 1777,	March 20, 1780.
James Moor,	Peterborough,	Feb. 15, 1777,	Dec., 1781.
Abel Merrill,	Washington,	April 1, 1777,	March 20, 1780.
Samuel Morrison,	Stoddart,	Jan. 1, 1777,	Dec. 1781.
Benjamin McAllister,*	Nottingham,	Jan. 1, 1777,	March 7, 1778.
Terence McCauley,	Concord,	Jan. 1, 1777,	Dec., 1781.
David Merrill,	Derryfield,	March 1, 1777,	Aug. 9, 1780.
John Merrill,	Concord,	Jan. 1, 1777,	Dec. 1781.

FIRST NEW HAMPSHIRE REGIMENT. 149

Name	Town	Date	Date
Andrew McIntire,	....	Feb. 7, 1777,........	Dec., 1781.
John McIntire,	Lyndeboro,	March 8, 1777,	March 20, 1780.
Nathaniel Moulton,	Deerfield,	Jan. 1, 1777,	Dec., 1781.
Timothy Martin,	Merrimack,	March 8, 1777,	March 20, 1780.
John Moors,	....	April 15, 1779,	Dec. 26, 1781.
Paul McCoy,	....	April 25, 1779,	Dec., 1781.
John McGinness,*	Nottingham,	Jan. 1, 1777,	June 17, 1778.
Cato Mercey,*	....	Jan. 26, 1777,	May 27, 1778.
William Metier,	Alstead,	Jan. 1, 1777,	Jan. 3, 1780.
John Metier,	Alstead,	Jan. 1, 1777,	Jan. 3, 1780.
Enoch Morse,	....	Feb. 2, 1777,	Dec., 1781.
John McClintock,	Goffestown,	March 15, 1777,	Nov. 1, 1780.
James Merrill, D.,*	....	April 1, 1778,	July 14, 1780.
Nathan Moulton,*	Alstead,	April 1, 1777,	June 2, 1778.
Robert Mason,	....	March 17, 1778,	Feb. 4, 1781.
Robert Miller,	....	Feb. 17, 1777,	Jan. 22, 1780.
John Manning,	....	Jan. 1, 1777,	Jan. 3, 1780.
John McClellen,	Chester,	April 1, 1777,	March 20, 1780.
Eliphalet Manning,	Dunstable,	April 15, 1777,	Dec., 1781.
Barnard Merrill,	Chester,	April 4, 1777,	April 4, 1780.
Joseph Marsh,	Henneker,	April 7, 1777,	April 4, 1780.
Thomas Matthews,*	Bedford,	April 25, 1777,	March 16, 1781.
James Mutchmore,	Pembroke,	Jan. 23, 1777,	Jan. 23, 1780.
Ichabod Martin,	Derryfield,	Jan. 1, 1777,	Dec., 1781.
Alexander McMasters,	Londonderry,	Jan. 1, 1777,	Dec., 1781.
Joseph Mack,	Londonderry,	April 2, 1777,	April 5, 1780.

150 HISTORY OF THE

Enlisted Men who served in the First New Hampshire Regiment — continued.

NAMES.	WHERE FROM.	WHEN ENTERED.	WHEN DISCHARGED.
Obed McLain,	Litchfield,	Jan. 1, 1777,	1780.
Joseph McFarland,	Londonderry,	Jan. 1, 1777,	April, 1780.
George McMurphy,	Londonderry,	Jan. 1, 1777,	April, 1780.
John McCoy,	Deerfield,	March 12, 1778,	Dec., 1781.
Daniel McCoy,	Deerfield,	March 15, 1778,	Dec., 1781.
Thomas McGlaughlin,	Deerfield,	March 12, 1778,	March 12, 1781.
Stephen McCoy,	Bow,	May 22, 1779,	Dec., 1781.
Ebenezer Matthews,	Claremont,	March 4, 1778,	Dec., 1781.
William McBritian,*		Feb. 16, 1777,	July 15, 1777.
Broadstreet Mason,	Nottingham,	Jan. 8, 1779,	Dec., 1781.
Isaac Mitchell,	Mason,	Jan. 1, 1777,	Sept. 1781.
Samuel Marsh,	Exeter,	Feb. 29, 1780,	Dec., 1781.
Jona Morgan,		Feb. 5, 1780,	Dec., 1781.
John Morgan,	Londonderry,	Jan. 1, 1780,	Dec., 1781.
Geo. Montgomery,	Gilmanton,	Feb. 10, 1781,	Dec., 1781.
Nehemiah Merrill,	Brintwood,	March 27, 1781,	Dec., 1781.
Hugh Moore,	Windham,	March 10, 1781,	Dec., 1781.
John Matthews,	Peterborough,	Jan. 1, 1777,	Dec., 1781.
Josiah Megoon,		April, 1781,	Dec., 1781.
Jonathan Morse,	Dublin,	April 24, 1781,	Dec., 1781.
Matthew Miller, D		Feb. 17, 1777,	Jan., 1779.
Josiah McLoon,*	Epping,	April 10, 1781,	Dec., 1781.

FIRST NEW HAMPSHIRE REGIMENT. 151

Benjamin Neley,	Meredith,	Jan. 1, 1777,	Sept. 19, 1777.
Nathaniel Needham,*	Wilton,	March 1. 1777,	Jan. 2, 1779.
Joseph Norris,	Deerfield,	March 4, 1778,	Feb. 4, 1781.
Timothy Newton,	Charlestown,	Jan. 1, 1777,	Dec., 1781.
William Nelle,	Exeter,	Jan. 1, 1777,	July, 1781.
Gains Niles,		Jan. 1, 1777,	Jan., 1781.
Samuel Neal,		1780,	Dec., 1781.
John Nicholson,		Sept. 6, 1781,	March 20, 1981.
Thomas Newnam,		March 1, 1777,	Dec., 1781.
James Orr,		March, 1777,	Dec., 1780.
Derrick Oxford,		May 3, 1777,	Dec., 1781.
Thomas Osgood,	Claremont,	Jan. 1, 1777,	Jan. 1, 1780.
John O'Brian. D.,	London,	April 7. 1777,	Dec., 1781.
Moses Ordway,	Lyndeboro,	1780,	Feb. 14, 1781.
William Pettegrew,		March 1, 1778,	Dec. 3, 1779.
Benjamin Pottingill,*	Epsom,	Jan. 1, 1777,	Jan. 2, 1780.
Benjamin Perkins,	Epping,	Jan. 1, 1777,	April 10, 1780.
Robert Parker,	Amherst,	April 9, 1777,	Jan. 25, 1780.
Nathaniel Patton,	Hollis,	Feb. 1, 1777,	Dec., 1781.
Daniel Putnam,	Cornish,	Feb. 12, 1777,	Dec., 1781.
Thomas Pratt,	Hollis,	Feb. 1, 1777,	Dec. 20, 1777.
William Pratt,*		April 18, 1777,	Dec., 1781.
Joel Proctor,	Hampstead,	March 15, 1778,	Jan. 25, 1780.
John Perry,		Feb. 19, 1777,	Jan. 20, 1780.
Jonathan Powers,	Dunstable,	Jan. 15, 1777,	June 20, 1780.
William Powell,	Dunstable,	June, 15, 1777,	

Enlisted Men who served in the First New Hampshire Regiment — continued.

NAMES.	WHERE FROM.	WHEN ENTERED.	WHEN DISCHARGED.
Joseph Polley,	Windham,	April 7, 1777,	April 10, 1780.
Davis Plummer, *	Londonderry,	April 7, 1777,	July 26, 1778.
Nathan Plummer,	Londonderry,	April 7, 1777,	April 10, 1780.
Jethro Pettingall,	Deerfield,	March 6, 1777,	Dec., 1781.
Abner Preston,	New Ipswich,	Feb. 1, 1777,	Jan. 21, 1780.
Simon Powers,	Ackworth,	May 5, 1777,	Dec., 1781.
Jona Pettingall,		April 16, 1777,	Dec., 1781.
Samuel Phelps,	New Ipswich,	Jan. 1, 1777,	Nov. 18, 1779.
William Prichard,	Nottingham,	Jan. 1, 1777,	Nov. 18, 1779.
John Pike,	Charlestown,	Jan. 1, 1777,	Jan., 1779.
Nathan Powers,	Richmond,	Jan. 1, 1777,	Dec., 1781.
Thomas Powers,	Richmond,	Jan. 1, 1777,	Dec., 1781.
Abner Powers, C.	Richmond,	Feb. 13, 1777,	Dec., 1781.
Noah Porter,		Jan. 1, 1778,	Dec., 1780.
Peter Phillips,		May 1, 1778,	July, 1781.
Samuel Potter,	New Ipswich,	Jan. 1, 1777,	Dec., 1781.
Thomas Barry,	Nottingham West,	April 12, 1779,	April 10, 1780.
Coleman Parker,	Portsmouth,	May 2, 1779,	Dec., 1781.
William Page,	London,	Jan. 1, 1777,	Dec., 1781.
John Putnam,	Lyndborough,	Feb., 1781,	Dec., 1781.
Benjamin Pierce,		Feb., 1781,	Dec., 1781.
Levi Pottle,	Wilton,	May, 1781,	Dec., 1781

FIRST NEW HAMPSHIRE REGIMENT.   153

Thomas Powers,		1781,	Dec., 1781.
Silas Porter,	Keene,	April, 1781,	Dec., 1781.
John Powell,		Jan. 9, 1777,	Dec., 1779.
Eliphalet Quimby,	Kingston,	April 4, 1777,	Dec., 1781.
Andrew Quimby,	Wakefield,	March, 1781,	Dec., 1781.
Ames Royce,*		May 1, 1777,	May 5, 1778.
Joel Royce,	Claremont,	May 1, 1777,	May 1, 1780.
James Kendall,	Nottingham,	Jan. 1, 1777,	
Zadok Reid,	Litchfield,	Jan. 4, 1777,	1781.
John Robertson,		Jan. 1, 1777,	1780.
Daniel Riter,*	Walpole,	Jan. 1, 1777,	Sept. 1, 1779.
James Rider, D		Jan. 1, 1777,	1780.
Richard Richardson,	Stoddart,	April 3, 1777,	April 5, 1780.
Richard Robinson,		Feb. 2, 1777,	Dec., 1781.
Nathaniel Richardson,*	Stoddart,	April 3, 1777,	June 24, 1777.
Richard Rogers, †		Feb. 25, 1777,	Sept. 19, 1777.
William Richardson,		Jan. 1, 1777,	Jan. 5, 1780.
Jonathan Rankin,*	Lyndeboro,	April 4, 1777,	March 28, 1778.
John Rowe,		April 15, 1777,	1780.
John Runell,*		Feb. 3, 1777,	Feb. 1, 1778.
James Riddle,	Bow,	March 23, 1777,	March 20, 1780.
John Reid,		May 17, 1777,	Dec., 1781.
James Russ, †	Chester,	Feb. 9, 1777,	Oct. 18, 1777.
John Riddle,	Deerfield,	March 7, 1778,	Feb., 1781.
Lemuel Rice,	Richmond,	Feb. 14, 1778,	Dec., 1781.
Paris Richardson,	Croydon,	Feb. 13, 1778,	Dec., 1781.

20

154 HISTORY OF THE

Enlisted Men who served in the First New Hampshire Regiment — continued.

NAMES.	WHERE FROM.	WHEN ENTERED.	WHEN DISCHARGED.
Asael Roundy, *	Lempster,	May 1, 1777,	Jan. 17, 1778.
Reuben Rogers,	Newmarket,	Jan. 1, 1777,	Dec., 1781.
Daniel Rogers, *	Rochester,	May 11, 1777,	July 20, 1777.
John Raino,	Amherst,	April 26, 1777,	Dec., 1781.
Nathan Rendall,	Nottingham,	Jan. 1, 1777	
Moses Roberts,		Feb. 28, 1780,	Dec., 1781.
William Rhines,	Canterbury,	1780,	Dec., 1781.
Silas Russell,	Perrystown,	April, 1780,	Dec., 1781.
John Rawlins,	Portsmouth,	Jan. 25, 1780,	Dec., 1781.
Asa Redington,	Wilton,	Feb. 27, 1781,	Dec., 1781.
Stephen Richardson,	FitzWilliam,	Feb. 23, 1781,	Sept. 1, 1781.
William Redfield,		Jan. 1, 1777,	April 5, 1781.
James Rouse, D		Feb. 1, 1777,	May 7, 1779.
James Seils,	Candia,	April 11, 1778,	Dec., 1781.
John Smith, S	New Boston,	April 5, 1777,	Dec., 1781.
Asa Stearns,	Claremont,	May 1, 1777,	Dec., 1781.
Ephraim Stevens, *		Feb. 15, 1777,	March 20, 1780.
Daniel Stearns, *	Claremont,	May 1, 1777,	April 30, 1780.
Peter Spicer,	Cornish,	May 1, 1777,	March 20, 1778.
Michael Silk, D	Jaffrey,	July 23, 1777,	Dec., 1781.
Thomas Sanderson,		April 1, 1777,	April 13, 1780.
Thomas Scott,	Amherst,	Jan. 1, 1777,	Dec., 1781.

FIRST NEW HAMPSHIRE REGIMENT. 155

John Stone,*	New Boston,	Feb. 12, 1777,	Sept. 6, 1777.
Samuel Smith,	Goffestown,	Jan. 20, 1777,	Dec. 1781.
Peter R. Stevens,	Boscawen,	Jan. 1, 1777,	Dec. 1781.
Ebenezer Sinclair,*	Weare,	Feb. 1, 1777,	Oct. 7, 1777.
Alexander Smith, C.	Brintwood,	Jan. 1, 1777,	Dec. 1781.
John Sanborn,	Barnstead,	April 1, 1777,	Sept. 10, 1778.
Brad Sinclair,*	Barnstead,	June 21, 1777,	March 5, 1778.
Joshua Sinclair,	Barnstead,	June 21, 1777,	June 20, 1780.
Samuel Sinclair,	Barnstead,	June 21, 1777,	June 20, 1780.
Ephraim Stevens,	Perryfield,	March 1, 1777,	Jan. 25, 1780.
William Shattuck,*	Boscawen,	Jan. 1, 1777,	June 20, 1777.
Isaac Smith,†	Amherst,	April 3, 1777,	April 10, 1780.
Jeremiah Suart,*		Feb. 2, 1777,	Oct. 7, 1777.
Isaac Stearns,		Jan. 1, 1777,	Jan. 7, 1778.
Jotham Stevens,		Feb., 1777,	Nov. 14, 1777.
Henry Stevens,		March 22, 1778,	April 5, 1780.
Edward Slapp,*		April 22, 1777,	Dec. 31, 1777.
David Sanderson,	Hollis,	Feb. 1, 1777,	Dec. 1781.
David Shirley,	Chester,	April 12, 1777,	April 5, 1781.
Benjamin Smith,	Lyndeboro,	March 14, 1777,	Dec. 1781.
David Smith,	Lyndeboro,	March 14, 1777,	Jan. 1, 1780.
William Stimpson,		May 9, 1779,	Dec. 1781.
Thomas Stickney,		Feb. 20, 1777,	Feb. 25, 1780.
Thomas Shrouder,*	Chester,	Dec. 19, 1776,	March 1, 1778.
Edward Smith,		April 17, 1777,	April 20, 1780.
Bartho Stevens,	Chester,	Feb. 1, 1777,	Feb. 1, 1780.

Enlisted Men who served in the First New Hampshire Regiment — continued.

Names.	Where From.	When Entered.	When Discharged.
Henry Snow,*	Portsmouth,	April 14, 1777,	Oct. 25, 1779.
John Sampson,		Jan. 1, 1777,	Dec., 1781.
William Simpson,		Jan. 1, 1777.	Jan. 1, 1780.
Nathaniel Shade,		May 14, 1779,	Dec., 1781.
Samuel Stone,*		Jan. 1, 1777,	Jan. 20, 1778.
William Sisco,	Croyden,	May 1, 1778,	Dec., 1781.
Samuel Sisco,	Newport,	Feb. 7, 1777,	Feb., 1780.
Ejhum Severance,*	New Ipswich,	Feb. 1, 1777,	Oct. 7, 1777.
James Simons, D.		Jan. 1, 1777,	Dec. 20, 1778.
John Simons,	Winchester,	Jan. 1, 1777,	Dec. 14, 1780.
Silas Simons,	Swansey,	Jan. 1, 1777,	Dec. 14, 1780.
Levi Simons,	Swansey,	Feb. 13, 1778,	Dec. 14, 1780.
Jona Smith,	Dunbarton,	April 4, 1777,	Oct. 26, 1777.
Samuel Stocker,	Hopkinton,	April 10, 1777,	March 7, 1780.
Joseph Sanborn,	New Market,	Jan. 1, 1777,	Nov. 18, 1779.
Thomas Severance,*	Hawke,	March 21, 1777	March 21, 1780.
John Swett,	Weare,	April 16, 1777,	April 20, 1780.
David Smith,*	Hopkinton,	April 10, 1777,	Aug. 4, 1778.
Elijah Suart,	Hopkinton,	April 7, 1777,	April 10, 1780.
Caleb Suart,	Hopkinton,	April 7, 1777,	April 10, 1780.
Benjamin Swett,*	Weare,	April 16, 1777,	April 20, 1780.
Jonathan Stevens,*	Dunbarton,	April 6, 1777,	May 25, 1778.

FIRST NEW HAMPSHIRE REGIMENT. 157

Name	Town	Enlisted	Discharged
Jona. Sawyer,	Hopkinton,	April 4, 1777,	April 5, 1780.
James Shearer,	Societyland,	April 6, 1777,	April 5, 1780.
Benjamin Smith,		Jan. 1, 1777,	Dec. 1781.
Roger Stevens,		April 18, 1777,	Dec. 1781.
Johnsen Smith, D.	New Boston,	April 5, 1777,	Nov. 6, 1778.
John Scott, D.		July 1, 1778,	Dec. 1781.
William Shaw, D.	Lyndeboro,	July, 1777,	Feb. 1778.
Stephen Seranton,		Feb., 1780,	Dec. 1781.
Daniel Sergeant,		May, 1780,	Dec. 1781.
Joseph Sudrich,		Feb. 5, 1780,	Dec. 1781.
Amos Snow,	Dover,	Dec., 1779,	Dec. 1781.
John Smith,		Oct., 1780,	Dec. 1781.
Michael Sutten,	Canterbury,	March, 1781,	Dec. 1781.
Henry Stevens,		March, 1781,	Dec. 1781.
Edward Spaulding,	Lyndeboro,	Feb., 1781,	Dec. 1781.
Luther Smith,		Feb., 1781,	Dec. 1781.
Peter Stevens,	Deerfield,	March, 1781,	Dec. 1781.
John Stone,	Dublin,	April, 1781,	Dec. 1781.
Moses Springer,		April, 1781,	Dec. 1781.
Benjamin Stone,	New Boston,	April, 1781,	Dec. 1781.
Merrill Sheppard,	Canterbury,	April, 1781,	Dec. 1781.
John Smith,	Salisbury,	March, 1781,	Dec. 1781.
Amos Spafford,	Peterborough,	Jan. 1, 1781,	Dec. 1781.
Robert Stevenson,		May, 1781,	Dec. 1781.
Samuel Saunders,	Salisbury,	March, 1781,	Dec. 1781.
John Still,	Walpole,	Feb., 1781,	Dec. 1781.

Enlisted Men who served in the First New Hampshire Regiment — continued.

Name.	Where From.	When Entered.	When Discharged.
Ebenezer Smith,	Brentwood,	Feb., 1781,	Dec., 1781.
Bernard Sargent,	Deerfield,	March, 1781,	Dec., 1781.
Isaac Stearns,	Rye,	March, 1781,	Dec., 1781.
Ebenezer Scribner,	East Kingston,	March, 1781,	Dec., 1781.
Tyler Spafford. D.		Feb., 1778,	April, 1780.
John Taggart,*	Peterborough,	Feb. 15, 1777,	July 7, 1777.
Jacob Taylor,	Hampton,	March 21, 1778,	Feb. 14, 1781.
Loring Thompson,		May 1, 1777,	May 1, 1780.
Hugh Thornton,*	Merrimack,	March 8, 1777,	March 1, 1778.
James Thompson,		March 1, 1777,	Dec., 1781.
Nathan Tuttle,		April 9, 1777,	April 10, 1780.
Seth Thompson,		April 18, 1777,	April 20, 1780.
Medad Taylor,		March 18, 1777,	Dec., 1781.
Jeremiah Towle,	Chester,	April 3, 1777,	April 3, 1780.
Henry True,	Chester,	April 3, 1777,	April 3, 1780.
Benjamin Taylor,	Dunstable,	April 17, 1777,	April 20, 1780.
Solomon Todd,	Londonderry,	April 28, 1777,	April 30, 1780.
James Thompson,	Chester,	Jan. 1, 1777,	Nov., 1779.
Abner Thustin,		Jan. 16, 1777,	Jan., 1781.
Joseph Tucker,	Swansey,	Feb. 3, 1778,	Dec., 1780.
Henry Thompson,	London,	Jan. 1, 1777,	Dec., 1781.
Ezra Turner,	Keene,	May 5, 1777,	April 20, 1777.

FIRST NEW HAMPSHIRE REGIMENT. 159

Name	Town		
Thomas Tuttle,*	Weare,	May 1, 1777,......	Feb. 17, 1778.
Prince Thompson,		May 15, 1777,......	May 17, 1781.
John Taylor, D	Antrim,	June 15, 1777,......	1778.
William Taggart,	Richmond,	Feb. 4, 1778,......	Dec., 1781.
Ezekiel Thurston,		March 8, 1781,......	Dec., 1781.
John Thomas,	New Ipswich,	March 13, 1781,......	Dec., 1781.
Francis Talbert,	Portsmouth,	Feb. 20, 1781,......	Dec., 1781.
Jonathan Thomas,	Sanbornton,	1781,.............	
William Thompson, D	Goffestown,	May 7, 1781,......	June 7, 1781.
John Vance,	Chester,	April 28, 1777,......	April, 1781.
John Wrine,	Boscawen,	1781,.............	Dec., 1781.
Jonathan Wheelock,	Peterborough,	May 1, 1777,......	May 1, 1780.
Abner Wise, C	Winchester,	Feb. 14, 1777,......	July 5, 1781.
Titus Wilson,*	Peterborough,	April 1, 1777,......	July 7, 1777.
William H. Wilkins,*	Candia,	April 11, 1778,......	June 22, 1778.
William White,	Washington,	Jan. 1, 1777,......	Jan. 1, 1780.
Joseph Wilson,	Lyndeboro,	Jan. 15, 1777,......	Dec., 1781.
Samuel Wier,	Jaffrey (Negro),	March 18, 1777,......	May 18, 1780.
Ebenezer Williams,	Candia,	March 10, 1778,......	1780.
Samuel Wells, S	Chester,	Jan. 1, 1777,......	Dec., 1781.
Samuel Whidden,	Merrimac,	March 8, 1777,......	March, 1780.
Peter Wells, C	Chester,	Jan. 1, 1777,......	Dec., 1781.
William Willey,	Nottingham,	Jan. 1, 1777,......	Dec., 1781.
Rufus Walton,	Alstead,	March 10, 1777,......	March 20, 1780.
Reuben Wheeler,	Amherst,	April 1, 1777,......	March 20, 1780.
George Wilson,	Amherst,	Feb. 3, 1777,......	Jan. 20, 1780.

Enlisted Men who served in the First New Hampshire Regiment — continued.

NAMES.	WHERE FROM.	WHEN ENTERED.	WHEN DISCHARGED.
Thomas Wilson,	Alstead,	Jan. 1, 1777,	Dec., 1781.
Silvester Wilkins,*		Feb. 1, 1777,	Nov. 7, 1777.
Lewis Wison,	Richmond,	Jan. 1, 1777,	Sept., 1781.
Joseph Wright,	Claremont,	Jan. 1, 1777,	April 1, 1780.
William Winton,		April 14, 1777,	Sept. 27, 1777.
Phineas Wright,		April 22, 1777,	April 23, 1780.
Jonathan Walker,*		April 18, 1777,	June 6, 1778.
Luther Wheatly,*		April 22, 1777,	Sept. 30, 1777.
Lebeus Wheeler,*	Hollis,	April 10, 1777,	July 10, 1778.
Jonathan Wright,	Lebanon,	April 22, 1777,	April 20, 1780.
Wilder Willard,	Plainfield,	April 21, 1777,	April 20, 1780.
David Wright,		March 17, 1778,	Feb. 14, 1781.
Paul Woods,	Dunstable,	April 1, 1777,	April 20, 1780.
William White,*	Chester,	April 1, 1777,	July 28, 1778.
Josiah Wells,*	Chester,	April 1, 1777,	July 31, 1778.
Daniel Woods,	Dunstable,	April 17, 1777,	April 20, 1780.
Robert Wilson,	Londonderry,	April 1, 1777,	March 20, 1780.
Samuel Walton,	Londonderry,	April 9, 1777,	April 10, 1780.
William Walker,	Canterbury,	June 3, 1777,	May 20, 1780.
James Wilson,	Greenland,	April 1, 1777,	May 20, 1780.
John Watts,*†		March 7, 1777,	Sept. 19, 1777.
Jonathan Wilson,		Jan. 1, 1777,	July 1, 1778.

FIRST NEW HAMPSHIRE REGIMENT.

			Furloughed.
Ithamar Wheelock,	New Ipswich,	Feb. 1, 1777,	Jan. 1, 1781.
Jonathan Webster, D.	Kingston,	March 7, 1777,	April 5, 1780.
Benjamin Williams,	Hopkinton,	April 6, 1774,	Jan. 31, 1779.
Stephen Ward, D.		Jan. 1, 1777,	Dec., 1781.
Thomas Watson,		April 6, 1780,	Dec., 1781.
James Winton,		Jan. 1, 1781,	Dec., 1781.
John Wallace,		March 27, 1778,	Dec., 1781.
Stephen White,	Fitz William,		Dec., 1780.
Benjamin Ward,		April, 1780,	Dec., 1781.
Joseph Wilson,		Jan. 1, 1780,	Jan. 1, 1780.
Thomas Whitock,		Jan. 1, 1777,	1781.
John Williams, D.		1781,	Dec., 1781.
Ezekiel York,	Brentwood,	1781,	July, 1777.
John Yarmon, D.	New Ipswich,	Jan. 1, 1777,	Dec., 1780.
Daniel Young,	Warner,	Jan. 27, 1778,	Dec., 1781.
Joseph York,	Nottingham,	March 1, 1777,	

Roll of Non-Commissioned Officers and Soldiers belonging to the First New Hampshire Regiment for the year ending December 31st, 1782.

Most of them are entered as commencing Jan. 1, 1782. Some few of them from March to August, the largest part of the former had belonged to the First or Third Regiment, but a reorganization seems to have taken place Jan. 1, 1781, and also Jan. 1, 1782. It is supposed most of them served through 1783 till the regiment was discharged. Those marked with a D deserted, * died, S Sergeant, C Corporal.

Samuel Allen,
John Ash,
Joseph Avery,
Aaron Adams,
David Abrahams,
Samuel Adams,
Beriah Abbott,
Isaac Adams,
Ebenezer Allen,
Samuel G. Allen,
David Adams, S,
William Aldridge,
Ami Andrews,
Joseph Avery,
John Allen,
Stephen Atkinson,
Timothy Abbott,
John Adams, C,
John Abbott,
James Aldds,
Josiah Breedy,
Jethro Barber,
Kies Bradley,
Joel Baker,
Daniel Bridges,
Samuel Boyd,
Asaph Butler,
Amos Baker,

Peter Bullard,
William Brown,
Enoch Badger,
John Bemus,
John Burk,
Aaron Basford, D, *
John Blanchard,
Andrew Bradford,
Benjamin Brown,
Benjamin Berry,
Jonathan Black,
Jonathan Banina,
Joseph Burk, S, * D,
Uriah Ballard, C,
Abner Bingham,
David Bryant, * D,
Stephen Bohonon,
Nathaniel Bean,
John Blaisdell, S,
Nathaniel Brown,
Charles Bowles,
Aaron Bigsbee,
Charles Branscombe,
Daniel Barker,
Nathaniel Barrott,
Hart Baltch,
Cesar Barnes,
Eleazer Ballard,

FIRST NEW HAMPSHIRE REGIMENT. 163

Simeon Butterfield,
Josiah Barton,
Samuel Brown,
Peter Bebee,
Ephraim Blood,
Jethro Barber,
Anniah Bohannon,
John Barton,
Naboth Batterson,
Isaac Cady,
Moses Cooper,
John Cooper,
Daniel Cook, S,
Eliphalet Cole,
John Cross,
Enoch Carleton,
James Cochran,
Abial Chandler,
Solomon Chapman,
Nathaniel Call,
Ebenezer Carleton,
Thomas Cochran,
Isaac Clemonds,
Daniel Colby,
Stephen Colby,
Hezekiah Colby,
Robert Cochran,
Joseph Chase,
Ebenezer Coster,
George Cooper, S,
Edmund Colby,
Salem Colby,
Moses Chandler,
Benjamin Creary,
Gilbert Caswell,
John Caldwell,
John Clark,

Robert Collins,
Bunker Clark,
Daniel Clough,
Abraham Currier,
Moses Colby,
Jonathan Cooper,
James Chamberlain,
Benjamin Cotten, S,
Theopalas Cass, S,
Moses Cutter,
Michael Chaplin,
Benjamin Crichett,
David Clark,
Robert Cunningham,
Benjamin Cressy,
Francis Como,
Moses Cutter,
John Dorman, C,
Joshua Danford,
Stephen Dustin,
Daniel Downing,
Daniel Dagin,
Benjamin Dockum,
Samuel Davis,
March Duty,
Ephraim Dudley,
Benjamin Dow, C,
Richard Drought,
Jarius Dickey,
Nathaniel Dickey,
Benjamin Dole,
John Dennis, D,
Nicholas Dodge,
James Dowd,
Charles Dorithy,
Zephaniah Downes,
Jonathan Eaton,

Peasley Eastman,
Jacob Eastman,
Daniel Emery,
Edward Evens,
John Eastman,
John Elaihnees, S,
Josiah Eastman,
George Emerson,
Joseph Ellison,
John Eaton,
James Eddy,
Henry Eastman,
Benjamin Ellis,
Jeremiah Fairfield,
Gideon Fletcher,
Jerre Foster,
Philip Flanders, D,
Joshua Fall,
Samuel Fuller,
Samuel Fugard,
Timothy Furnham, S,
John Farnham, C,
Jacob Flanders,
Nathan Foster,
Offen French,
Thomas Fuller,
Isaac Farwell,
Jeremiah Fogg,
Ebenezer Fosgood,
Jacob Gile,
Nathaniel Grimes,
David Greeley,
Seth Gow,
Ephraim Goss,
Peter Goss,
James Gipson,
Henry Gipson,

John A. Goss,
Joseph Gilman,
John Grow,
Daniel Gold, C,
Daniel Gage,
John Greeley,
Joseph Gray,
Joseph Green,
Benjamin Grace,
John Gault,
Jonathan Griffin,
Hugh Gorgan,
Mathew Green,
Bradbury Green,
William Glines,
Nathaniel Glines,
John Grout,
Michael George,
John Gaffit,
James Gordon,
Solomon Gibson,
David Haskell,
Benoni Hill,
Zacheus Hunt,
Buckley Hutchins,
Moses Hutchins,
David Hunt, C,
Moses M. Howe,
Simon Hinowh,
David Howe, S,
Joseph Hoit,
Peter Henry,
Moses Heath, *
John Head,
Cato Hale,
Thomas Haines,
William Howit,

FIRST NEW HAMPSHIRE REGIMENT.

William Haywood,
James Hawley,
Israel Hale,
Joseph Howe,
Ephraim Hildreth,
Thomas Harvey,
Thomas Holmes,
Israel Howe, S,
Daniel Holt, C,
Reuben Horsmore,
David Howard,
Stephen Hermon,
Joel Holt,
Wiliam Hamlet,
Joseph Hodgman,
Aaron Hays,
Ebenezer Hoey,
Joseph Houghton,
William Hardy,
William Hubbard,
John Hall,
Joseph Heman,
Robert Hastings,
Robert Hemphill,
Jonathan Hazeltine, D,
Moses Heath,
Moses Hutchins,
William Hewitt,
John Humble,
Levi Hoit,
Daniel Harper,
Joseph Horman,
Solomon Hazeltine,
Solomon Harris,
Thomas Hunt,
Samuel Hoit, C,
Nathan Hoit,
David Johnson, S,
Philip Johnson, Jr.,
Philip Johnson,
Edward Jones,
William Jones,
Taylor Joslin,
John Jennes,
Asa Jackson,
Jeremiah Johnson,
John Kent,
Thomas Kimball,
David Kinnerton,
Reuben Kidder,
Reuben Keasor, D,
Jonathan Kelly,
William Kimball,
Daniel Kimball,
Ebenezer Kinneston,
Robert Livingston, S,
Samuel Lyon,
John Lovering,
William Leaton,
John Larrabee,
Noah Levins,
Samuel Lock, C,
Moses Lock,
Nehemiah Leavitt,
John Lapish,
Isaac Lowell,
William Lowell,
John Louring, D,
Timothy Lock,
Andrew Law,
Benjamin Lamper,
William Lakin,
Josiah Magoon,
James Martin, D,

Eliphalet Manning, C,
Enoch Morse,
Samuel Morrison,
John Morgan.
Nathaniel Molten,
John Manning, S,
Broadstreet Mason, C,
Ichabod Martin, C,
George Montgomery,
Daniel McCoy,
Stephen McCoy,
Obed McLane,
Andrew McIntire, D,
Elkin Moore,
Jonathan Molton,
Nehemiah Merrill, L,
John McLaughlin,
William Morling,
Hugh Moore,
George McGolpin,
Jonathan Miller,
Paul McCoy,
Flourance McCulley,
Ezra Merriam,
Edward Mardeen, C,
James Moore,
Ebenezer Matthews, S,
Thomas McNeal, S,
John Matthews,
Enoch Morse,
Moses Moore,
James Moore,
John Moore,
Isaac Mitchell,
Elkin Moore,
Abel Merrill,
Jonathan Morse,

Jacob Morse,
Jonathan McCoy,
Jonathan Morgan,
John Merrill,
Samuel Marsh,
David Nicholson, D,
James Nokes,
Timothy Newton,
David Nevins, S,
John Nicholson,
Mark Nutter,
John Night,
Abraham Night,
Gaus Niles,
Thomas Osgood,
James Orr,
Abner Powers, C,
Jethro Pettengill,
Nehemiah Philips,
John Peabody,
Thomas Peabody,
Nathaniel Powers, C,
Simeon Powers, C,
Thomas Powers,
Silas Porter,
Moses Powers,
Colburn Parker,
Stephen Putney,
Jonathan Putney,
John Purple, C,
Thomas Pitts,
Ichabod Perry,
Benjamin Pierce,
Daniel Putnam,
Asa Pudney,
Thomas Pratt,
Levi Pottle,

FIRST NEW HAMPSHIRE REGIMENT. 167

Ezekiel Proctor,
Adam Patterson,
Benjamin Powell,
Jonathan Pettingill,
Amasa Parker,
Benjamin Perry,
Joel Proctor,
Isaac Patterson,
Eliphalet Quimby, S,
Andrew Quimby, *
Alexander Ronalds,
Abram Ronalds,
John Rollings,
Joseph Rollings,
Lemuel Richardson,
Stephen Richardson, C,
Asa Redington,
Jeduthen Roberts,
Eliphalet Rollings,
Solomon Rathburn,
Benjamin Roby,
Moses Reed, D,
Zadoc Read,
Paris Richardson,
Samuel Rendall,
Ezekiel Rooks,
Moses Roberts,
Nathaniel Randall,
John Reed,
Samuel Royce,
Isaac Royce,
Silas Russell,
Richard Robinson, S,
Moses Springer,
Jeduthen Roberts,
Reuben Roberts,
John Still,

Samuel Smith,
Darius Sneed,
Mathew M. Sanburn,
Peter R. Stevens,
John Smith, *
Benjamin Sanburn,
James Sales,
Jacob Schegell, *
Benjamin Smith,
John Sampson,
Stephen Scranton,
Henry Stevens,
Nathan Stevens,
John Smith, S,
Roger Stevens,
Benjamin Short,
Edward Spaulding,
Luther Smith,
Abel Sargents,
Henry Smith,
Joseph Spaulding,
William Sisco, *
Peter Stevens,
Stephen Spaulding,
Samuel Spaulding,
Moses Springer,
William Simpson,
Michael Sutten,
Benjamin Smith,
John Stone,
Josiah Simpson,
Jeremiah Smith,
Nathan Shade,
Barnard Sargents,
Ebenezer Smith,
Alexander Smith,
Benjamin Smith,

William Scott, S,
Amos Spofferd,
Joseph Sudwick,
Robert Stetterson, *
John Shepard, C,
Daniel Sargent,
Robert Sargent,
Henry Shaw,
Peter Stevens,
Benjamin Stone,
Merritt Shepard,
Amos Snow,
Michael Silk,
Isaac Stearns,
Israel Spencer,
David Sanderson,
Ebenezer Scribner,
Samuel Sanders,
James Taylor,
Henry Tibbitts,
John Trask,
William Taggart,
William Temple,
Joseph Tucker,
Henry Thompson,
Ezekiel Thirston,
Jacob Thomas,
Stephen Thomas,
Samuel Trickey,
John Taylor,
Jonathan Thomas,
Abraham Thompson,
John Thomas,
Adolph Temple,
Thomas Tuttle, *

John Trickey,
Medad Taylor,
Jeremiah Tylor,
Jonathan Urin,
James Vinton,
John Wadleigh,
Joseph Wilson, *
John Wilson, *
John Wolcott, *
Edward West,
Thomas Watson,
Matthew Worthington, *
Peter Walls, S,
William Willey, C,
Nathaniel Whitcombe,
Benjamin Ward,
Jacob Weatherbee, *
Isaac Wilkins,
Thomas Wilson,
Lewis Wisso,
Rupha Watters,
Joseph Willson,
John Wallis,
Silas Whitney,
Abner Wise,
Abraham Wetmore, S,
Daniel Wilson,
Andrew White,
Stephen White,
Thomas Welch,
John Youngman,
Samuel York,
Ezekiel York,
Jabez Youngman,
Joseph York.

INDEX.

Abbott, Beriah, 162.
Abbott, John, 162.
Abbott, Captain Joshua, 10.
Abbott, Stephen, 131.
Abbott, Timothy, 131, 162.
Abraham, David, 131, 162.
Adam, Samuel, 131, 162.
Adams, Aaron, 131, 162.
Adams, David 131, 162.
Adams, Elisha, 131.
Adams, Lt. J, 86, 88.
Adams, Isaac, 131.
Adams, John, 84, 131, 162.
Adams, Jonas, 131.
Adams, Levi, 132.
Aiken, James, 131.
Aiken, Samuel, 131.
Albany, 24.
Albany, march to, 37.
Albany, winter at, 76.
Aldds, James, 162.
Aldrich, Nathan, 132.
Aldridge, William, 162.
Aldds, Isaac, 131.
Allen, Surgeon's Mate David, 85.
Allen, Ebenezer, 131, 162.
Allen, John, 162.
Allen, John, D., 131.
Allen, Samuel, 131, 162.
Allen, Samuel G., 131, 162.
Allowance, to officers, 86.
Alstead, 118.
Americans, 24.
Ames, Francis, 131.
Amherst, 119, 130.
Amoskeag Falls, 90.
Amwell, march to, 38.
Anderson, Second Lieut. James, 10.
Andre, captured, 55.
    hanged, 56.
Andrews, Ami, 162.
Andrews, Joel, 131.
Andrews, Nathaniel, 132.

Appletown, march to, 52.
Arnold, Gen., joined the army, 30, 33.
Arnold, plot discovered, 55.
Ash, John, 131, 162.
Ashely, Daniel, 132.
Atkinson, First Lieut. Samuel, 10.
Atkinson, Stephen, 162.
Averil, Elijah, 131.
Avery, Joseph, 162.

Bacon, Lieut., 86.
Badger, Enoch, 162.
Bailey's, regiment, 35.
Baker, Amos, 133, 162.
Baker, Joel, 132.
Balcarras, Earl of, 22.
Baldwin, Captain Isaac, 10.
Baldwin, John, 133.
Baldwin's, regiment, 125.
Ballard, Eleazer, 162.
Ballard, Uriah, 162.
Baltch, Hart, 162.
Banina, Jonathan, 162.
Barber, Jonathan, 162.
Barber, Jethro, 133, 162, 163.
Barker, Daniel, 132, 162.
Barlow, John, 133.
Barnes, Cesar, 162.
Barnet, Benjamin, 134.
Barnet, Lieut. Robert, 84.
Barrett, Nathaniel, 132, 162.
Barron, John 133.
Barron, Lt. Oliver, 88.
Barrons, Samuel, 133.
Bartlet, John, 133.
Bartlet, Nathaniel, 133.
Barton, John, 163.
Barton, Josiah, 163.
Basford, Aaron, 162.
Basson, Jonathan, 101.
Batchelder, Nathaniel, 132.
Batchelder, William, 133.

INDEX.

Bates, Nathaniel, 134.
Bates, Samuel, 133.
Bates, Thomas, 133.
Batterson, Naboth, 163.
Baxter, Thomas, 134.
Beadle, Col., 108.
Bean, Nathaniel, 162.
Behee, Peter, 163.
Bedford, march to, 44.
Beede, Bezia, 132.
Bell, C. H. Esq., 128.
Bemis's heights, 33.
Bemirs, John, 162.
Bennington, militia come in, 33.
Berry, Benjamin, 134, 162.
Berry, Ebenezer, 134.
Berry, John, 132.
Berwick, 103.
Bevens, Benjamin, 133.
Beverly, James, 133.
Bigsbee, Aaron, 162.
Billings, Christopher, 133.
Bingham, Abner, 134, 162.
Bingham, Ripley, 134.
Biographical sketches of officers, 90.
Bishop, Enos, 134.
Bishop, John, 134.
Black, Jonathan, 132, 162.
Blaisdell, John, 162.
Blake, Ensign Thomas, 12, 13.
   his commission, 14.
Blake, Lieut. and Pay-Mr. Thomas, 78, 82, 88.
   his Journal, 25, 57, 74, 115, 124.
   died, 126.
Blake, Patience, 124.
Blake, Samuel, 124.
Blake, William, 124.
Blake and Jackson, 126.
Blanchard, Col. 111.
Blanchard, Lt. James, 85.
Blanchard, John, 162.
Blanchard, Jonathan, 13, 17.
Blodgett, Lt. Caleb, 85, 86.
Blodgett, Joshua, 133.
Blood, Asa, 132.
Blood, Daniel, 134.
Blood, Ephriam, 101, 132, 163.
Bounties paid in silver, 79.
Bowles, Charles, 132, 162.
Bowles, James, 133.
Boxford, 126.
Boyd, Second Lieut. Nathan, 10.
Boyd, Samuel, 133, 162.
Boyes, James, 132.

Boynton, Adjt. J. 88.
Boynton, Isaac, 134.
Boynton, Lieut. Joseph, 85, 86.
Bradbury, Sanders, 134.
Bradford, Andrew, 162.
Bradford, Lieut. William, 130.
Bradley, Keys, 102, 132, 162.
Branscomb, Charles, 132, 162.
Brant Life of, 33.
Brant, Stone's life of, 30.
Breedy, Josiah, 162.
Brewer, Peter, (Negro) 134.
Bridges, Daniel, 162.
Bristol, 5.
British army at Locust hill, 39.
British defeated at Saratoga, 36.
British deserters, 32.
Brown, Benjamin, 134, 162.
Brown, James, 133.
Brown, John, 133.
Brown, Moses, 133.
Brown, Nathaniel, 162.
Brown, Samuel, 163.
Brown, Scipio, 135.
Brown, William, 132, 134, 162.
Brunswick, march to, 43.
Bryant, David, 133, 162.
Bryer, Peter, 134.
Bohannon, Anniah, 132, 163.
Bohanon, Stephen, 162.
Bonney, Jacob, 133.
Boston, evacuation of, 3.
Bounties for enlistments, 17.
Bounty to soldiers, 75.
Boutwell, Asa, 133.
Bugbee, Nathaniel, 134.
Burgoyne's surrender how celebrated, 45.
Bullard, Peter, 133, 162.
Bullock's house, 47.
Bunker, Clark, 163.
Bunker hill, 129.
Bunker hill, New Hampshire troops at, 3, 4.
Burk, John, 162.
Burk, Joseph, 133, 162.
Burns, Caesar, 134.
Burrows, Jonathan, 133.
Burton, Josiah, 132, 134.
Burts, Robert, 134.
Buswell, Noah, 134.
Butler, Alpheus, 134.
Butler, Asaph, 162.
Butler, Benjamin, 134.
Butler, Col., ascends Cayuga lake, 53.

INDEX. 171

Butler, Col., his forces, 51.
Butler, John, 132.
Butterfield, Simeon, 135, 163.

Cadwallader, Gen., 5, 6.
Cady, Curtiss, 14, 135.
Cady, Isaac, 163.
Calcott, Isaac, 137.
Caldwell, John, 9, 135, 163.
Caldwell, Sergt. major, Samuel, 84, 136.
Call, Nathaniel, 163.
Cambell, James, 135.
Cambridge, British march to, 37.
Cammet, Thomas, 136.
Campbell, Drum Major James, 84, 136.
Canada, the regiment ordered to 3, 4.
Canandaigua, march to, 52, 53.
Cannon captured, 35.
Capron, Thomas, 137.
Captains, list of 1782., 81.
Carlton, Ebenezer, 163.
Carleton, Enoch, 163.
Carr, Major, 86.
Carr, Major, James, biog. sketch of, 109.
Carr, Second Lieut. Jesse, 10.
Carter, Edward, 135.
Carter, Ensign Hubbard, 83.
Cass, Capt. Jona., 81, 120.
Cass, Lewis, 120.
Cass, Lt. Jonathan, 185.
Cass, Major James, 85, 88.
Cass, Theophilas, 135, 163.
Castleton, retreat to, 28, 29.
Casualties, 82.
Caswell, Eliphlet, 137.
Caswell, Gilbert, 137, 163.
Cayuga lake ascended, 53.
Chadwick, John, 136.
Challis, Enos, 136.
Chamberlin, James, 137, 163.
Chandler, Abiel, 9, 10, 137, 163.
Chandler, Moses, 163.
Chaplin, Michael, 163.
Chapman, Solomon, 135, 163.
Charlestown, 117, 119, 130.
Charlestown, No. 4, 19, 25.
Chase, Joseph, 163.
Chase, Moses, 135, 137.
Chase, Surgeon's mate Josiah, 10.
Chemung, captured and destroyed, 49.
Cheny, Captain, Samuel, 85.

Chester, 118, 130.
Child, Cypril, 137.
Church, Thomas, 136.
Cilley, Col. Joseph, 21, 22, 23, 74, 82, 83, 103, 120.
 killed, 104.
 biog. sketch of, 93.
 died, 99.
Cilley's regiment, 11, 35, 47.
Cilley, Lieut. Jonathan, 85, 95, 120.
Cilley, Thomas, 93.
Clapp, Lieut. Daniel, 81, 83.
 Capt. Daniel, 119.
Clark, Bunker, 136.
 David, 163.
 Hezekiah, 137.
 John, 135, 136, 163.
 Josiah, 135.
 Thomas, 135.
Claverack, march to, 38.
Clemands, Isaac, 163.
Clements, Isaac, 137.
Clinton's brigade, 50.
Clothier, general, 63.
Clothing, destitution of, 72,
 prices of, 62.
 regulations for the army, 57.
Clough, Daniel, 137, 163.
Coburn, Rowlins, 137.
Cochran, James, 136, 163.
Cochran, Jonathan, 135.
Cochran, Robert, 163.
Cochran, Thomas, 163.
Cogan, Quarter Mr. Patrick, 84.
Colbie, Zebulun, 136.
Colburn, John, 137.
Colburn, Thomas, 135.
Colby, Daniel, 137, 163.
Colby, Edmund, 137.
Colby, Hezekiah, 163
Colby, Moses, 163.
Colby, Salem, 137, 163.
Colby, Stephen, 137, 163.
Cole, Eliphlet, 137, 163.
Collins, Benjamin, 136.
Collins, Ebenezer, 137.
Collins, Robert, 163.
Combs, John, 135.
Companies, list of in 1782, 81.
Como, Francis, 137, 163.
Conant, Jonathan, 135.
Concord, 116, 117.
Concord, battle of, 1.
Connell, William, 135.
Connely, Mr. 108.
Conner, John T., 136.

Constitution island encamp on, 56.
Continental army, 41.
Continental troops, each clothing, 75.
Cook, Daniel, 163.
Cook, William, 135.
Cook's regiment, 35.
Cooper, George, 163.
Cooper, John, 136, 163.
Cooper, Jonathan, 163.
Cooper, Moses, 163.
Corell's ferry, 38, 41.
Corliss, 2d Lieut. Jonathan, 10.
Cornwallis, capture of, 73.
Coster, Bishop, 135.
Coster, Ebenezer, 163.
Cotton, Benjamin, 135, 165.
Conno, Francis, 137.
Court House, 47.
Courtland's regiment, 35, 47.
Cowdrey, John, 135.
Cranberry town, march to, 42.
Crawford, Robert, 135.
Creesy, Daniel, 136.
Cressy, Benjamin 137, 163.
Critchett, Benjamin, 136, 137, 163.
Cross, Ephraim, 136.
Cross, John, 136, 163.
Cross, Thomas, 137.
Croton bridge, march to, 44.
Crown point, 111.
Crown point road, 19.
Crumpond, march to, 54.
Cunningham, Robert, 135, 136, 163.
Currier, Abraham, 163.
Currier, Alva, 137.
Currier, Jonathan, 135.
Curtiss, Timothy, 136.
Cutter, Moses, 137, 163.
Cutting, Jonas, 137.

Dagin, Daniel, 163.
Dale, Benjamin, 139.
Dale, John, 138.
Danbury, march to, 45, 46.
 winter at, 54.
Danford, Joshua, 138, 163.
Danford, Samuel, 139.
Davis, Ezekiel, 138.
Davis, John, 138.
Davis, Joseph, 138.
Davis, Nathan, 138.
Davis, Samuel, 139, 163.
Davis, Thomas, 138.
Dayne, Jacob, 138.
Dean, Lemuel, 138.

Dearborn, Col. 21, 86.
 ascends Cayuga lake, 55.
 General H. A. S., 101.
 Col. Henry, biog. sketch of, 100.
 Capt. Henry, 10.
 Henry, 101.
 Godfrey, 100.
 Lt. Col. 74, 85.
 Lt. Col. in command, 78.
 Second Lt. Samuel, 10.
Dearborn's company, 118.
 regiment, 35.
Deaths in regiment, 131.
Deerfield, 128.
DeKalb, Maj. Gen., 44.
Delaware river, crossed, 38.
Dennis, John, 163.
Depreciation of paper currency, 80.
Derryfield, 121.
Deserters from British, 32, 36.
Dickey, Benjamin, 139.
Dickey, David, 138.
Dickey, James, 138.
Dickey, Jarius, 163.
Dickey, Nathaniel, 138, 163.
Dickey, William, 139.
Discharges, time of, 131.
Dockum, Benjamin, 139, 163.
Dodge, Nicholas, 139, 163.
Dodge, Thomas, 139.
Dole, Benjamin, 163.
Donop, Count, 5.
Door, John, 138.
Dorchester, Mass., 124.
Dorman, John, 139, 163.
Dorthy, Charles, 163.
Dougherty, Charles, 138.
Douglass, John, 139.
Dover, 104.
Dow, Benjamin, 138, 163.
Dowd, James, 139, 163.
Downing, Daniel, 163.
Down, Zephaniah, 139, 163.
Drought, Richard, 138, 163.
Ducit, Philemon, 138.
Dudley, Ephraim, 163.
Dulton, Samuel 138.
Dumbarton, 124.
Duncan, Thomas, 138.
Dunnell, Reuben, 138.
Dunstable, 111.
Durrah, Wm. 138.
Dustin, Capt. Moody, 81, 86, 88.
 biog. sketch of, 114.
 Lieut. Moody, 82.

INDEX. 173

Dustin, Stephen, 139, 163.
Dury, March, 163.
Dwire, John, 138.

East Concord, 128.
East Hampton, 105.
Eastman, First Lt. Ebenezer, 10.
Eastman, Henry, 140, 164.
Eastman, Jacob, 139, 164.
Eastman, John, 164.
Eastman, John, Sr, 139.
Eastman, John, Jr, 139.
Eastman, Jonathan, 139.
Eastman, Joseph, 139.
Eastman, Josiah, 140, 164.
Eastman, Peasley, 164.
Eastman, Samuel, 140.
Easton, Penn., march to, 47.
Easton, return to, 54.
Eaton, John, 140, 164.
Eaton, Jonathan, 163.
Eddy, James, 164.
Edgar hill, 28.
Elailmees, John, 164.
Ellingwood, Ralph, 139.
Elliott, John, 139.
Ellis, Capt. Benjamin, 81, 85, 164.
Ellison, Joseph, 140, 164.
Emerson, Capt. Amos, 81, 82, 118.
    George, 164.
    Ralph, 113, 139.
    killed, 114.
Emery, Daniel, 140, 164.
Emery, Noah, 140.
English army, 80.
Englishtown, march to, 42, 43.
Enlisted men, 1777 to 1782, 131.
Enlistments, encouragements of, 16, 17.
Epsom, 105, 118.
Evans, chaplain, 45.
Evans, Edward, 139, 164.
Evans, Ira, 139.
Evans, Stephen, 13, 17.
Exeter, 100, 111, 120, 128.
    convention at, 1, 2.
    sends supplies, 19.
Eyers, Samuel, 139.

Fairfield, Elijah, 140.
Fairfield, Jeremiah, 164.
Fall, Joshua, 141, 164.
Farmer & Moore's *Collections*, 130.
Farmington, march to, 46.
Fermoy, Brig. Gen., 26.
Farnham, Timothy, 141, 164.

Farnham, John, 164.
Farnham, John S., 140.
Frankford, Wm, 140.
Farnsworth, Moses, 140.
Farwell, Capt. Isaac, 81, 82, 109, 164.
Farwell's Company, 129.
Field officers, 1780, 82.
First New Hampshire regiment,
    first so called, 3.
    ill condition of, 4.
    in battle Trenton, 6.
    in battle Princeton, 8, 9.
    roll of officers, 9.
    at battle Bunker hill, 11.
    reorganized, 11.
    served in Delaware, 13.
    Cilley colonel of, 21, 95.
    at Ticonderoga, 21, 27.
    retreat from Ticonderoga, 28.
    at Stillwater, 32.
    at Saratoga, 22, 31, 34.
    return, of loss by battle, 35.
    ordered to attack British, 36.
    march to Albany, 37.
    mutiny, 38.
    crossed Delaware, 38, 41.
    join Washington's army, 38.
    at Valley Forge, 40.
    sickness, 41.
    pursues British in Jersey, 41.
    battle of Monmouth, 42.
    winter at Redding, 46.
    capture and destroy Chemung, 49.
    invade Seneca country, 50.
    battle Newtown, 51.
    winter near Danbury, 54.
    led against mutineers, 72.
    2d and 3d regiments merged in, 74.
    death of Col. Scammell, 74.
    under Lt. Col. Dearborn, 74.
    badly clothed, 75.
    hutted at New Windsor, 76.
    had repose, 76.
    last regiment disbanded, 77.
    served eight years and eight months, 77.
    ask for grant of land, 78.
    unsuccessful therein, 79.
    mode of drawing pay, 80.
    roll of officers, 81.
    effective force, 81.
    casualties and promotions, 82.
    allowance to officers, 86.

First New Hampshire regiment,
　pay of officers and men, 87.
　in service Jan. 1784, 88.
　accounts of, 89.
　biog. sketches of officers, 90.
　reduced by casualties, 97.
　enlisted men, 1777 to 1782, 131.
Fishkill, march to, 38.
Five mile point, 26.
Flanders, Jacob, 140, 164.
Flanders, John, 140.
Flanders, Philip, 140, 164.
Fletcher, Gideon, 141, 164.
Fletcher, Phineas, 141.
Fogg, Jeremiah, 164.
Folsom, Gen., 2, 3.
　difficulty with Stark, 93.
　Col. Nathaniel, 1.
Forgtae, Ebenezer, 140.
Form of Enlistment, 14.
Forrest, Robert, 140.
Fort Ann, 29.
Fort Edward attacked, 30.
　army arrived at, 31.
　retreat to, 29.
Fort George taken, 101.
Fort Miller, 30, 31.
　retreat to, 29.
Fort Stanwix, march to, 32, 33.
Fosgood, Ebenezer, 164.
Foster, Ephraim, 140.
Foster, Jerre, 164.
Foster, Nathan, 141, 164.
Fosto, Antonio, 140.
Fourth July, celebrated, 43, 48.
France, news of alliance, 41.
Frankford, W. M., 140.
French Katharine's, 52.
French lines, 29.
French, Offen, 164.
French, war, 25.
Frost, Elpir, 140.
Frothingham's Siege of, 41.
Frink, Surgeon's mate Calvin, 10.
Frye, Captain, 86.
Frye, Capt. Ebenezer, 67, 81, 82.
　biog. sketch of, 116.
　1st Lt. Ebenezer, 10.
　Capt. Isaac, 81, 85, 88.
　biog. sketch of, 115.
Frye's company, 128.
Fugard, Samuel, 140, 164.
Fuller, Daniel, 140.
Fuller, Samuel, 164.
Fuller, Thomas, 140, 164.
Fuzier, William, 141.

Gaflit, John, 164.
Gage, Daniel, 142, 164.
Gaghaheywarahera, march to, 53.
Gardinier, Surgeon Nathaniel, 82.
　biog. sketch of, 105.
Gates, Gen. in command, 33.
Gates's army celebrate anniversary
　Burgoyne's surrender, 45.
Gault John, 142, 164.
Genesee, Castle destroyed, 53.
Genesee, river forded, 53.
George, Benjamin, 141.
George, Isaac, 141.
George, Michael, 164.
George, Thomas, 141, 142.
German convention troops on the
　march to Virginia, 46.
German troops defeated, 36.
Gibbs, David, 141.
Gibbs, Isaac, 141.
Gibbs, Joshua, 141.
Gibson, Solomon, 164.
Gile, Jacob, 164.
Giles, Benjamin, 13, 17.
Gill, Silas, 141.
Gillman, Josiah, Jr., 83.
Gilman, Anthony, 142.
Gilman, D., 13, 17.
Gilman, Lt. Col. Jeremiah, 82, 104.
　biog. sketch of, 105.
Gilman, Joseph, 142, 164.
Gilman, Major, 107.
　promoted, 21.
Gilmore, James, 141.
Gilmore, Thomas, 141.
Gipson, Henry, 164.
Gipson, James, 164.
Gleason, Wilson, 142.
Glines, Nathaniel, 141, 164.
Glines, William, 142, 164.
Godle, William, 141.
Godle's regiment, 106.
Gold, Daniel, 164.
Gold, Moses, 141.
Gold, Nehemiah, 141.
Goodale, Asa, 141.
Gordon, James, 164.
Gorgan, Hugh, 164.
Goss, Ephraim, 164.
Goss, John Abbott, 142, 164.
Goss, Peter, 164.
Gould, Daniel, 142.
Gould, Lieut. James, 84.
Gould, Simeon, 141.
Goult, George, 141.
Goush, Thomas, 141.

INDEX. 175

Gow, Seth, 164.
Grace, Benjamin, 164.
Grace, Benjamin W., 142.
Grafton county, recruiting in, 12.
Graham, Nathaniel, 144.
Grant, Duncan, 144.
Grant, Joseph, 144, 142.
Gray, Joseph, 164.
Grear, Matthew, 142.
Greeley, David, 164.
Greely, John, 142, 164.
Green, Bradburry, 164.
Green, Joseph, 164.
Green, Mathew, 164.
Green, Maj. Gen., 55, 56.
Greenbush, march to, 55.
Greenfield, Charles, 142.
Gregory, William, 142.
Griffin, John, 142.
Griffin, Jona. 142, 164.
Grimes, Nathaniel, 164.
Groat, John, 142, 164.
Grow, John, 142, 164.
Guffet, John, 142.
Gulph mills, march to, 40.

Hadley, Joseph, 143.
Haines, Thomas, 145, 164.
   bravery of, 23, 24.
Hale, Cato, 143, 164.
Hale, Israel, 143, 165.
Hale, Rev. John, 82, 105.
   biog. sketch of, 110.
Hale, First Lieut. John, 10.
Hale, Col. Nathan, his regiment, 35, 109.
Hale, William, 145.
   biog. sketch of, 112.
Hall, Dr., 100.
Hall, John, 145, 165.
Hamlet, William, 165.
Hampshire, regiment, 36.
Hancock, John, 16, 62.
Hand's brigade, 49.
Hanneyauyen, march to, 52, 53.
Hanover, 119.
Hardy, James, 145.
Hardy, Nathaniel, 145.
Hardy, 1st. Lieut. Thomas, 10.
Hardy, William, 165.
Harper, Daniel, 143, 165.
Harper, John, 144.
Harper, Samuel, 143.
Harper, Thomas, 143.
Harriman, Paye, 145.
Harris, Henry, 144.

Harris, Solomon, 144, 165.
Hart, Balch, 132.
Hartford, march to, 46.
Hart's regiment, 144.
Harvey, Lt. John, 85.
Harvey, Thomas, 143, 165.
Haskell, David, 164.
Hastings, Robert, 165.
Hastings, Sylvanus, 143.
Haverstraw, march to, 56.
Hawley, James, 145, 165.
Hayes, Aaron, 143, 165.
Hays, Nathaniel, 145.
Haywood, William, 165.
Hazeltine, Solomon, 165.
Hazelton, John, 144.
Hazilton, Jere, 144.
Hazleton, Jonathan, 144, 165.
Hazleton, Joseph, 144.
Head, John, 145, 164.
Heath, Gen., 75, 76.
Heath, Jesse, 145.
Heath, Moses, 143, 164, 165.
Heath, William, 101.
Heman, Joseph, 165.
Hemington, Timothy, 145.
Hemphill, Robert, 165.
Henderson, Joseph, 143.
Henry, Peter, 145, 164.
Henry's Mass. regiment, 107.
Herman, Stephen, 165.
Herod, James, 145.
Hessians captured, 40.
Hessians in New Jersey, 5.
Hessians surrender at Trenton, 7.
Hewett, Wm., 143, 165.
Hews, Samuel, 144.
Hickey, Barabas, 144.
Hildreth, Ephraim, 143, 165.
Hill, Benoni, 143, 164.
Hill, David, 143.
Hill, Samuel, 144.
Hills, Ebenezer, 144.
Hills, Joseph, 144.
Hillsborough, 130.
Hillsgrove, John, 144.
Hilton, John P., 143.
Hinowh, Simon, 164.
Hodgart, Robert, 145.
Hodgkins, Wm., 142.
Hodgman, Joseph, 144, 165.
Hoey, Ebenezer, 144, 165.
Hogg, George, 144.
Hoit, Enoch, 142.
Hoit, Joseph, 164.
Hoit, Joseph B., 143.

INDEX

Hoit, Levi, 145, 165.
Hoit, Nathan, 165.
Hoit, Samuel, 145, 165.
Holcomb, Matthew, 143.
Holland, Robert, 143.
Holland, Capt., 103.
Hollis, 111, 113.
Holman, Jeremiah, 145.
Holmes, Thomas, 165.
Holt, Asa, 145.
Holt, Daniel, 143, 165.
Holt, Joel, 144, 165.
Homan, Joseph, 143, 165.
Honey, Calvin, 145.
Hopewell, march to, 42.
Hopkinton, 117.
Horsmore, Reuben, 165.
Houghton, Joseph, 165.
House, Capt. John, 42.
Howard, David, 165.
Howard, Roswell, 144.
Howe, David, 143, 164.
Howe, Joseph, 165.
Howe, Lieut. Bezaleel, 83, 86, 88, 130.
Howe, Moses M., 164.
Howes, Israel, 143, 165.
Howit, William, 164.
Hoyt, Lieut. Nathan, 85.
Hoyt, Second Lieut. Stephen, 10.
Hubbard, William, 165.
Hubbardston, Hale's regiment broken up at, 109.
Hubbarton, 28.
Hubbart, Jonas, 144.
Hudson, Benj., 143.
Hudson, regiment at, 74.
Hull, Major, 96.
Humble, John, 143, 165.
Humphreys, Col., 74.
Hunt, David, 145, 164.
Hunt, Thomas, 114, 143, 165.
Hunt, Zacheus, 145.
Huntington's regiment, 41.
Hutcherson, Elijah, 144.
Hutcherson, Levi, 144.
Hutchins, Capt. Gordon, 10.
Hutchins, Capt. Nathaniel, 81, 82. biog. sketch of, 117.
Hutchins, Moses, 145, 165.
Hutchins, Simeon, 144.
Hutchins's company, 118.
Hutchinson, John, 145.
Hutchinson, Timothy, 145.
Huts erected at Redding, 46.
Huts erected at Valley Forge, 40.

Huts removed from, 41.
Huts erected for winter, 54, 56.
Huts rafted down the river, 31, 32.

Independence, how celebrated, 43, 48.
Indian depredations, 30, 31.
Indians, attacks by, 26, 27, 31.
Indians killed, 51.
Indian towns, expedition to destroy, 117.
Ingalls, Israel, 146.
Irvine, Gen., 5.

Jackson, Asa, 146, 165.
Jackson's regiment, 35.
Jacob's Plains, 47.
Jay, John, 14.
Jenkins, Peter, 146.
Jennens, Ephraim, 146.
Jennens, John, 145, 165.
Jennens, Stephen, 146.
Jersey redoubt, 28.
Jerseys, British marched to, 41.
Jeverich, march to, 55.
Johnson, David, 146, 165.
Johnson, Jeremiah, 165.
Johnson, Philip, 165.
Johnson, Philip, Jr., 165.
Johnson, Thomas, 146.
Joiner, Francis, 146.
Joiner, John, 146.
Joiner, Quarter Master Sergeant John, 84.
Jones, Edward, 165.
Jones, Quarter Master Sergeant John, 85.
Jones, William, 165.
Jorden, John, 146.
Judkins, Joel, 146.
Judkins, Jona., 145, 146.
Judkins, Philip, 146.
Judkins, Drum Major Samuel, 85.

Kanadasaga, march to, 52, 53.
Keasor, Reuben, 165.
Kelley, Jonathan, 147, 165.
Kelsey, Giles, 147.
Kemp, William, 146.
Keneghses, march to, and attack by Indians, 52.
Keneghises, march to, 53.
Kenney, Amos, 146.
Kent, John, 146, 165.
Kent, march to, 46.
Kidder, Daniel, 146.

INDEX. 177

Kidder Reuben, 147, 165.
Kimball, Lieut. and Pay-Master Benj., 84, 125.
Kimball, Daniel, 165.
Kimball, Thomas, 146, 165.
Kimball, William, 147, 165.
Kinderhook, march to, 38.
King's ferry, march to, 38, 44, 54.
Kingsley, Alpheus, 146.
Kingston, Mass., 102.
Kingstown, march to, 42.
Kinnerton, David, 165.
Kinneston, Ebenezer, 165.
Kinsman, Capt. Aaron, 10.
Kirkeat, march to, 44.
Knock, Jona. 147.
Knott, Jesse, 146.
Knowles, Samuel, 146.
Knox, Gen., special agent to enforce Washington's appeal, 72, 146.
Knox, George, 146.
Knox, Samuel, 147.
Kondar, march to, 52.
Kosciusko, Gen., 96.

Lakawaneck, march to, 48.
La Fayette, Gen., commands detachment, 42, 129.
Lakin, William, 148, 165.
Lamb, James, 147.
Lamper, Benjamin, 165.
Lang, William, 148.
Lansingburgh, 32.
Lany, John, 148.
Lapish, John, 147, 165.
Larrabee, John, 147, 165.
Larrabee, Samuel, 147.
Latimer's regiment, 35.
Law, Andrew, 148, 165.
Lawrence, Ensign Joseph, 84.
Lawrence, Lieut. Joseph, 130.
Layton, William, 147.
Learned's brigade, 44.
Leaton, William, 165.
Leavitt, Nehemiah, 165.
Lee, Gen., 42.
Lee, Lieut. William, 84, 130.
Lee, Samuel, 147.
Lee's division, 41.
Leonard's brigade, 35, 132.
Leving, John, 148.
Levins, Noah, 148, 165.
Lewey, William, 147.
Lexington, battle of, 1.
Light Infantry, loss at Saratoga, 35.

Lincoln, Gen., 109.
Lines, Charles, 147.
Liscomb, Samuel, 147.
Litchfield, 114.
Little, First Lieut. Moses, 10.
Livermore, Capt. Daniel, 81, 85, 86, 88, 116.
  his journal, 117.
Livermore, Second Lt. Daniel, 10.
Livingston, Robert, 165.
Livingston Manor, march to, 38.
Livingston's regiment, 35.
Lock, Moses, 147, 165.
Lock, Orson, 147.
Lock, Samuel, 147, 165.
Lock, Timothy, 148, 165.
Locust Hill, British at, 39.
Locust Hill, march to, 47.
Londonderry, 90, 110, 119, 128.
Longfellow, Bradberry, 93.
Longfellow, Jonathan, 93.
Longfellow, Sarah, 93.
Long's regiment, 117.
Lord, Stephen, 147.
Lormington, march to, 38.
Lossing's Field Book Revolution, 37.
Louring, John, 165.
Lovejoy, Abel, 147.
Lovejoy, Asa, 147.
Lovell, Icabod, 147.
Loverin, John, 147, 165.
Lowdon's ferry, 32.
Lowell, William, 148, 165.
Loyns, Michael, 147.
Lufkin, Levi, 148.
Lund, William, 147.
Lyndeborough, 130.
Lyon, Samuel, 165.

Mack, Joseph, 149.
Magoon, Josiah, 165.
Mahone, Philip, 148.
Manchester, 90.
Manning, Eliphalet, 149, 166.
Manning, John, 149, 166.
Mardeen, Edward, 166.
Marsh, Joseph, 149.
Marsh, Samuel, 150, 166.
Martin, Ichabod, 149, 166.
Martin, James, 165.
Martin, Timothy, 149.
Mason, Broadstreet, 150, 166.
Mason, Sergt. Major Edward, 85.
Mason, Lt. Lemuel, 85.
Mason, Robert, 149.

Massachusetts Bay aided by New Hampshire, 1.
Matthews, Ebenezer, 150, 166.
Matthews, John, 150, 102, 166.
Matthews, Thomas, 149.
McAllister, Benj., 148.
McBritian, William, 150.
McCaulley, Lieut. Nathaniel, 84
McCaulley, Terence, 148.
McClary, Major Andrew, 9.
McClary Second Lieutenant Michael, 10.
McClellen, John, 149.
McClintock, John, 149.
McClintock, Chaplain Samuel, 10.
McCoy, Daniel, 150, 166.
McCoy, John, 150.
McCoy, Jonathan, 166.
McCoy, Paul, 149, 166.
McCoy, Stephen, 150, 166.
McCulley, Flourance, 166.
McFarland, Joseph, 150.
McGee, John, 149.
McGee, William, 149.
McGinness, John, 149.
McGlaughlin, Thomas, 150.
McGolpin, George, 166.
McIntire, Andrew, 149, 166.
McIntire, John, 149.
McLain, Obed, 150, 166.
McLocu, Josiah, 150.
McLaughlan, First Lieutenant Thomas, 10.
McLaughlin, John, 166.
McMasters, Alexander, 149.
McMurphy, George, 150.
McNeal, Thomas, 148, 166.
Medford, regiments quartered at, 3.
Megoon, Josiah, 150.
Mendon, 102.
Menow, Lieut., 86.
Mercer, Gen., 8.
Mercey, Cato, 149.
Merriam, Ezra, 166.
Merrill, Abel, 148, 166.
Merrill, Major Amos, 85.
Merrill, Barnard, 149.
Merrill, David, 148.
Merrill, James, 149.
Merrill, John, 148, 166.
Merrill, Nehemiah, 150, 166.
Merrill, Lieut. Simon, 150.
Merrimac, 90.
Milford, Mass., 102
Miller, Jonathan, 166.
Miller, Matthew, 150.

Miller, Robert, 149.
Millett, John, 148.
Mills, Ens. and Adj. Joseph, 82.
Mills, Lieut. Joseph, biog. sketch of, 128.
Mitchell, Isaac, 150, 166.
Molton, Jonathan, 166.
Molton, Nathaniel, 166.
Monmouth, battle of, 42.
  number of dead buried, 43.
Montgomery, Gen, 150, 166.
Moor, James, 148.
Moore, Capt. Daniel, 10, 116.
Moore, Elkin, 166.
Moore, Hugh, 150, 166.
Moore, James, 166.
Moore, John, 149, 166.
Moore, Capt. John, 10.
Moore, Maj. John, 9.
Moore, Second Lieut. John, 10.
Moore, Moses, 166.
Morgan, Col., 22, 33.
  attacked British, 39.
Morgan, John, 150, 166.
Morgan, Jona., 150, 166.
Morgan's regiment, 35.
Morgan's riflemen, 42.
Morling, William, 166.
Morrell, Maj. Amos, 85, 115.
  biog. sketch of, 148.
  Capt. Amos, 81, 82.
  First Lieut. Amos, 10.
Morrill, Lieut. Simon, 83.
Morris, Robert, 75.
Morrison, Samuel, 148, 166.
Morristown, march to, 38.
Morrow, Lieut. S., 88.
Morse, Enoch, 149, 166.
Morse, Jacob, 166.
Morse, Jonathan, 150, 166.
Moultin, Nathanael, 149.
Moulton, Nathan, 149.
Mount Defiance, 28.
Mount Hope, 27, 28.
Mount Independence, 25, 28, 29.
Moylan, J., clothier general, 68.
Munn, Nathan, 148.
Munn, William, 148.
Munro, Lieut. and Quarter Master Josiah, 82.
Munro, Capt. Josiah, 81, 119.
Mutchmore, James, 149.
Mutiny of Pensylvania line, 72.

Neal, Samuel, 151.
Neals, Mr., 31.

INDEX. 179

Needham, Nathaniel, 151.
Neley, Benjamin, 151.
Nelle, William, 151.
Nestor of the regiment, 113.
Nevins, David, 166.
New Antrim, march to, 38.
Newburg, 76.
New City, 32.
New Hampshire, called upon for
   3 regiments, 12.
  forces, ask for grant of land,
    78.
  line, 115.
  men early in the service, 1.
  regiments draw clothing, 76.
  survey for map of, 163.
  village (on the Hudson), 83.
New Hartford, march to, 46.
New Ipswich, 126.
New Jersey militia, 5.
  term of regiment expired in, 3.
  troops mutiny, 72.
Newman, Thomas, 151.
New Milford, march to, 46.
Newton, Timothy, 151, 166.
Newtown, battle of, 51.
  winter at, 54.
New Windsor, 77.
  regiment at, 80.
  regiments hutted at, 76.
New York and Vermont at strife,
   76.
  evacuated, 77.
  troops join Gen. Poor's bri
    gade, 32.
  troops receive grant of land,
    78.
  the regiment ordered to, 3.
Nicholson, David, 166.
Nicholson, John, 151, 166.
Night, Abraham, 166.
Night, John, 166.
Niles, Gains, 151, 166.
Nokes, James, 166.
Norfolk, march to, 46.
Norris, Joseph, 150.
North Castle, march to, 44.
North river, march to highlands
  on, 47.
Nottingham, 93, 120.
Number Four (Charlestown), 19,
   25.
Nutter, Mark, 166.

O'Brian, John, 151.
Officers, 81, 82.

Old Colony Club, 102.
Oneida Indians come in, 50.
Orangetown, march to, 55.
Ordway, Moses, 151.
Orr, James, 151, 166.
Osgood, Chaplain David, 9.
Osgood, Thomas, 151, 166.
Oxford, Derrick, 151.

Page, Capt. Caleb, 121.
Page, Elizabeth, 121.
Page, Ensign Moses, 85.
Page, William, 152.
Pampton, march to, 38.
Paper currency, scale of deprecia
  tion, 80.
Parker, Amasa, 167.
Parker, Colburn, 166.
Parker, Coleman, 152.
Parker, Robert, 151.
Parkinson, Qr. Master Henry, 9.
Parry, Thomas, 152.
Patten, Nathaniel, 151.
Patterson, Adam, 167.
Patterson, Isaac, 167.
Patterson's brigade, 44.
Pay of officers and men, 87.
Pay roll, Dec. 31, 1782, 85.
Pay rolls, 130.
Peabody, Thomas, 166.
Peekskill Landing, march to, 44,
   54.
Pembrooke, 116.
Pennsylvania, line mutiny, 72.
Pennsylvania regulars, 5.
Pensions, 19.
Peramus, march to, 41, 55.
Perkins, Benjamin, 151.
Perkins, Ensign Jona., 83.
Perry, Benjamin, 167.
Perry, Ichabod, 166.
Perry, John, 151.
Peterborough, 105, 107, 129.
Pettegrew, William, 151.
Pettingall, Jethro, 152, 166.
Pettingall, Jona., 152, 167.
Pettingill, Benjamin, 151.
Phelps, Samuel, 152.
Philadelphia, American army en-
  ter, 42.
  evacuated by British, 41.
  march to, 38.
  the regiment at, 3.
Philips, Nehemiah, 166.
Philips, Peter, 152.
Pierce, Benjamin, 152, 166.

Pike, John, 152.
Pitts, Thomas, 166.
Plimpton, encamped at, 54.
Plummer, Davis, 152.
Plummer, Nathan, 152.
Plymouth, 102.
Pocoma, march to, 47.
Polley, Joseph, 152.
Pool, Eleazer, 113.
Pool, Jonathan, (Surgeon's mate) 82.
    Biog. sketch of, 113.
Poor, Enoch, made colonel, 12.
Poor, Col., 18, 19.
Poor, Gen., 21, 22, 26, 92, 93, 95, 128.
    gives entertainment 4th July, 48.
Poor's Brigade, 32, 35, 37, 40, 44, 45, 46, 50, 51.
    regiment, 41.
Porter, Noah, 152.
Porter, Silas, 153, 166.
Portsmouth, 102.
Potter, Capt. Joseph, 85, 86, 88.
Potter, Samuel, 152.
Potter, Judge, 11.
Potter's history of Manchester, 4, 23.
Pottle, Levi, 152, 166.
Poughkeepsie, march to, 38.
Powell, Benjamin, 167.
Powell, John, 153.
Powell, William, 154.
Powers, Abner, 152, 166.
Powers, Jonathan, 154.
Powers, Moses, 166.
Powers, Nathan, 152.
Powers, Nathaniel, 166.
Powers, Simon, 152, 166.
Powers, Thomas, 152, 153, 166.
Pratt, Thomas, 154, 166.
Pratt, William, 154.
Prescott, Col., 111.
Preston, Abner, 152.
Prichard, Paul, 126.
Prichard, William, 129, 152.
Princeton, battle of, 8, 9.
Prisoners liberated, 44.
Pritchard, Lieut. and Adj. Jeremiah, 82.
    biog. sketch of, 126.
Proctor, Ezekiel, 167.
Proctor, Joel, 154, 167.
Promotions, 82.
Pudney, Asa, 166.

Purple, John, 166.
Putnam, Daniel, 14, 151, 166.
Putnam, John, 152.
Putney, Jonathan, 166.
Putney, Stephen, 166.

Quimby, Andrew, 153, 167.
Quimby, Eliphalet, 153, 167.
Quilutanuck, march to, 48.

Raino, John, 154.
Ralle, Col., 5, 6, 7.
Randall, Nathaniel, 167.
Rankin, Jonathan, 153.
Rathburn, Solomon, 167.
Rawlins, John, 154.
Read, Zadoc, 167.
Redding, march to, and wintered at, 46.
Redfield, William, 154.
Redington, Asa, 154, 167.
Redner, troops at, 40.
Reed, First Lieut. Abraham, 10.
Reed, James, made colonel, 2.
Reed, John, 167.
Reed, Moses, 167.
Reed's regiment at battle Bunker hill, 5.
Regiment, minimum standard of, 89.
Regimental clothier, 65.
    regulations, 80.
Regiments united, 97.
Reid, Col., 86, 118.
Reid, Lieut. Col. George, 85.
    in command, 78.
    biogr. sketch of, 110.
Reid, Capt. George, 10.
Reid, John, 153.
Reid, Zadok, 153.
Reid's company, 122.
    regiment, 103, 106, 115, 119.
Rendall, James, 153.
Rendall, Nathan, 154.
Rendall, Samuel, 167.
Rhinebeck, march to, 38.
Rhines, William, 154.
Rhode Island, 44.
Rice, Lemuel, 153.
Richards, Capt. Samuel, 10.
Richardson, Lemuel, 167.
Richardson, Nathaniel, 153.
Richardson, Paris, 153, 167.
Richardson, Richard, 153.
Richardson, Stephen, 154, 167.
Richardson, William, 153.

INDEX. 181

Riddle, James, 153.
Riddle, John, 153.
Rider, James, 153.
Ridgburry, march to, 54.
Ridgefield, march to, 44.
Riedesel, memoirs of Gen., 29.
Riflemen, loss at Saratoga, 35.
Riter, Daniel, 153.
Roberts, Juduthen, 167, 169.
Roberts, Moses, 154, 167.
Roberts, Reuben, 167.
Robertson, John, 153.
Robinson, Richard, 153, 167.
Roby, Benjamin, 167.
Rockingham county, 110.
Rogers, Daniel, 154.
Rogers, Reuben, 154.
Rogers, Richard, 153.
Roll of officers, 81.
Rollings, Eliphalet, 167.
Rollings, John, 167.
Rollings, Joseph, 167.
Ronalds, Abram, 167.
Ronalds, Alexander, 167
Rooks, Ezekiel, 167.
Rosse, James, 154.
Roundy, Asael, 154.
Rowe, John, 153.
Royal, Col., 122.
Royalton, attack on, 13.
Royce, Amos, 153.
Royce, Isaac, 167.
Royce, Joel, 153.
Runell, John, 153.
Russ, James, 153.
Russell, Silas, 154, 167.

Sales, James, 167.
Sampson, John, 156, 167.
Sanborn, Benjamin, 167.
Sanborn, John, 155.
Sanborn, Joseph, 156.
Sanborn, Mathew M., 167.
Sanders, Samuel, 168.
Sanderson, David, 155, 168.
Sanderson, Thomas, 154.
Saratoga, British at, 33.
   Battle of, 34.
Saratoga, march to, 31.
Saratoga falls, 31.
Saratoga, winter at, 76.
Saratoga, second battle, 36, 37.
Sargent, Bernard, 167, 168.
Sargent, Daniel, 168.
Sargent, Paul Dudley, made colonel, 2.

Sargent, Robert, 168.
Sargents, Abel, 167.
Sartwell, Capt. John, biog. sketch of, 117.
Sartwell, Capt. Lieut., 82.
Sartwell, Capt., 119.
Saunders, Samuel, 157.
Sawyer, Jona., 157.
Scammell, Col. Alexander, 18, 21, 63, 66, 85, 93, 98, 103, 104.
   inscription on tombstone, 74.
   made colonel, 12.
   biog. sketch of, 102.
Scammell's regiment, 35.
Schegell, Jacob, 167.
Schenectady, winter at, 76.
Schuyler, General, 26.
Schuyler papers, 78.
Schuylkill, foraging on, 39, 40.
Scott, Gen., 42.
Scott, Alexander, 105.
Scott, Fife Major John, 85, 157.
Scott, Thomas, 154.
Scott, Maj. William, 82, 86, 106, 108, 168.
Scott, Major, in command, 78.
Scott, Major William, biog. sketch of, 105.
Scott, Captian William, 107.
Scranton, Stephen, 157, 167.
Scribner, Ebenezer, 158, 168.
Second New Hampshire regiment, 74, 110.
Seils, James, 154.
Seneca country invaded, 50.
   lake, encampment at, 52.
   lake, march to, 53.
Senter, Capt. Asa, 84, 85, 86, 119.
Senter, Lieut. Asa, 83.
Sergeant, Daniel, 157.
Severance, Epham, 156.
Severance, Thomas, 156.
Shade, Nathan, 167.
Shade, Nathaniel, 156.
Shattuck, William, 155.
Shaw, Henry, 168.
Shaw, William, 157.
Shearer, James, 157.
Shepard, John, 168.
Shepard, Merritt, 168.
Sheppard, Merrill, 157.
Shesheek, march to, 49.
Shirley, David, 155.
Short, Benjamin, 167.
Shrouder, Thomas, 155.
Silke, Michael, 154, 168.

Simons, James, 156.
Simons, John, 156.
Simons, Levi, 156.
Simons, Silas, 156.
Simpson, Josiah, 167.
Simpson, William, 156, 167.
Simsbury, march to, 46.
Sinclair, Brad, 155.
Sinclair, Ebenezer, 155.
Sinclair, Joshua, 155.
Sinclair, Samuel, 155.
Sisco, Samuel, 156.
Sisco, William, 156, 167.
Slapp, Edward, 155.
Smart, Caleb, 156.
Smart, Elijah, 156.
Smart, Jeremiah, 155.
Sneed, Darius, 167.
Smith, Alexander, 155, 167.
Smith, Benjamin, 155, 157, 167.
Smith, David, 155, 156.
Smith, Ebenezer, 158, 167.
Smith, Edward, 155.
Smith, Henry, 167.
Smith, Isaac, 155.
Smith, Jeremiah, 167.
Smith, John, 154, 157, 167.
Smith, Jona., 156.
Smith, Johnson, 157.
Smith, Luther, 157, 167.
Smith, Samuel, 155, 167.
Snow, Amos, 157, 168.
Snow, Henry, 156.
Soldiers Fortune, winter at, 56.
  orders bought up, 101.
Somersworth, 109.
Soper, First Lieut. Joseph, 10.
Sortwell, Capt. Simon, 81.
South Canaan, march to, 46.
Spaulding, Edward, 157, 167.
Spaulding, Joseph, 167.
Spaulding, Samuel, 167.
Spaulding, Stephen, 167.
Spencer, Israel, 168.
Spencer's regiment, 47.
Spicer, Peter, 154.
Spofford, Amos, 159, 168.
Spafford, Tyler, 158.
Spotwood, march to, 43.
Springer, Moses, 157, 167.
Springfield, march to, 44.
Staff officers, 1780, 82.
  not to be clothed, 59.
Standingstone, march to, 49.
Stanwix, 32.
Stark, Archibald, 85, 90.

Stark, Adj. Caleb, 11, 84.
  died, 123.
  biog. sketch of, 124.
Stark, John, 2, 9, 13, 18, 19, 75, 76,
  78, 116, 121.
  at battle Trenton, 6.
  letter to the legislature, 29.
  ordered to report, 3.
  died, 93.
  biog. sketch of, 90.
  life of, 37.
Stark's at battle Bunker hill, 3.
  ordered to New York, 3.
  regiment, 125.
State clothiers, 65.
St. Clair, Gen., 26.
Stearns, Asa, 154.
Stearns, Daniel, 154.
Stearns, Isaac, 155, 158, 168.
Stearns, Jotham, 155.
Stetterson, Robert, 168.
Steuben, Maj. Gen., 44.
Stevens, Bartho., 155.
Stevens, Ephraim, 154, 155.
Stevens, Henry, 155, 157, 167.
Stevens, Jonathan, 156.
Stevens, Nathan, 167.
Stevens, Peter, 157, 167, 168.
Stevens, Peter R., 155, 167.
Stevens, Roger, 157, 167.
Stevens, Sergt., 7.
Stevenson, Robert, 157.
Stickney, Thomas, 155.
Still, John, 157, 167.
Stillwater, march to, 32, 33.
Stimpson, William, 155.
Stocker, Samuel, 156.
Stockton, Doctor, 86.
Stockton, Surg. Ebenezer, 85.
Stone, Benjamin, 157, 168.
Stone, John, 155, 157, 167.
Stone, Samuel, 156.
Stone Arabia, march to, 55.
Stony Point, 114, 115.
Storterdam, march to, 44.
Sudrich, Joseph, 157, 168.
Sullivan, Gen., 103.
  at battle Trenton, 6.
  near Philadelphia, 40.
  to command western army,
    47.
  the regiment under, 3.
  account of battle Newtown,
    51.
  expedition, 120.
Supplies for troops ordered, 1, 2.

INDEX.

Sutten, Michael, 157, 167.
Sweed's ford, march to, 39.
Sweet, Benjamin, 156.
Swett, John, 156.

Taggart, Lieut. James, 84.
Taggart, John, 158.
   biogr. sketch of, 129.
Taggart, William, 159, 168.
Talbert, Francis, 159.
Tappan, march to, 55.
Taylor, Benjamin, 158.
Taylor, Jacob, 158.
Taylor, James, 168.
Taylor, John, 159, 168.
Taylor, Joslin, 165.
Taylor, Medad, 158, 168.
Temple, Adolph, 168.
Temple, William, 168.
Third New Hampshire regiment, 14, 116, 120.
Thomas, Jacob, 168.
Thomas, John, 159, 168.
Thomas, Jonathan, 159, 168.
Thomas, Stephen, 168.
Thompson, Abraham, 168.
Thompson, Charles, 16, 60, 68.
Thompson, Ensign Samuel, 83.
Thompson, Henry, 158, 168.
Thompson, James, 158.
Thompson, Loring, 158.
Thompson, Lieut. Joshua, 83, 86, 88.
   biogr. sketch of, 128.
Thompson, Prince, 159.
Thompson, Seth, 158.
Thompson, William, 159.
Thornton, Hugh, 158.
Three mile point, 26, 27.
Thurston, Ezekiel, 159, 168.
Thustin, Abner, 158.
Tibbitts, Henry, 168.
Ticonderoga, 31, 109.
   supplies sent to, 19.
   two battalions to be raised at, 16.
   road to made in French war, 25.
   retreat from, 28.
   loss at, 29.
Tioga, march to, 49, 50, 54.
Titcomb, Lieut. Col. Benjamin, 82.
   biogr. sketch of, 104.
Toasts, 4th July, 1779, 48.
   at celebration of Burgoyne's surrender, 45.

Todd, Solomon, 158.
Tories captured, 29.
   in Butler's army, 51.
Towle, Jeremiah, 158.
Towne's company, 126.
Trask, John, 168.
Trenton, battle of, 6.
Trickey, John, 168.
Trickey, Samuel, 168.
True, Henry, 158.
Tucker, Joseph, 158, 168.
Tunkhannick, march to, 47, 49.
Turner, Ezra, 158.
Tuttle, Nathan, 158.
Tuttle, Thomas, 159, 168.
Tylor, Jeremiah, 168.

Urin, Jonathan, 168.

Vance, John, 159.
Valley-forge, encampment at, 10.
Vanderlip's farm, 49.
Van Schaick's island, 32.
Varnum's regiment, 41.
Verplanck's point, 76.
Vinton, James, 168.
Virginia, march to, 73.

Wadleigh, John, 168.
Wagoners not to be clothed, 59.
Wait, Capt. Jason, 81, 82.
Wait, Major Jason, 118.
Walker, Jonathan, 160.
Walker, William, 160.
Wallace, John, 161.
Wallis, John, 168.
Walls, Peter, 168.
Walpole, 130.
Walton, Rufus, 159.
Walton, Samuel, 160.
Ward, Benjamin, 161, 168.
Ward, Stephen, 160.
Washington, Gen., 41, 42, 55.
   appeals to regiment to remain in service, 4.
   at Newburgh, 76.
   entered New York, 77.
   the regiment under command of, 3, 4.
Watertown, 116.
Watson, Thomas, 161, 168.
Watters, Rupha, 168.
Watts, John, 160.
Weare, Lt. Nathan, 85.
Weare, Mesheech, 72.
Weatherbee, Jacob, 168.

Webster, Jonathan, 161.
Welch, Thomas, 168.
Wells, Josiah, 160.
Wells, Peter, 159.
Wells, Lt. Samuel, 85, 159.
West, Edward, 168.
West point, march to, 54, 56.
Wetmore, Abraham, 168.
Wheatly, Luther, 160.
Wheeler, Libeus, 160.
Wheeler, Reuben, 159.
Wheelock, Ithamar, 161.
Wheelock, Jonathan, 159.
Whidden, Samuel, 159.
Whitcombe, Nathaniel, 168.
White, Andrew, 168.
White, Stephen, 161, 168.
White, William, 159, 160.
White Marsh, march to, 38.
White Plains, march to, 44.
Whitehall, or Skenesboro', 29.
Whitney, Silas, 168.
Whitock, Thomas, 161.
Wier, Samuel, 159.
Wilkins, Isaac, 168.
Wilkins, Lieut. Robert B., 24.
Wilkins, Silvester, 160.
Wilkins, William H., 159.
Willard, Lieut. and Quarter Mast. Jona., 82, 130.
Willard, Wilder, 160.
Willet, Col., 74.
Willey, William, 159, 168.
Williams, Benjamin, 161.
Williams, Ebenezer, 159.
Williams, John, 161.
Williams, Surg. Obadiah, 10.
Williamsburg, monument to Col. Scammell at, 74.
Willson, Joseph, 168.
Wilmington, troops at, 40.

Wilson, Daniel, 168.
Wilson, George, 159.
Wilson, James, 160.
Wilson, John, 168.
Wilson, Jonathan, 160.
Wilson, Joseph, 159, 161, 168.
Wilson, Robert, 160.
Wilson, Thomas, 160, 168.
Wilson, Titus, 159.
Wilton, 115.
Winter hill, regiments stationed at, 3.
Winton, James, 161.
Winton, William, 160.
Wise, Abner, 159, 168.
Wisso, Lewis, 160, 168.
Woburn, 113.
Wolcott, John, 168.
Woodbury, Capt. Elisha, 10.
Woods, Daniel, 160.
Woods, Paul, 160.
Worthington, Matthew, 168.
Warwick, march to, 38.
Wright, David, 160.
Wright, Jonathan, 160.
Wright, Joseph, 160.
Wright, Phineas, 160.
Wrine, John, 159.
Wyman, Lieut. Col. Isaac, 9.
Wyoming, march to, 54.

York, Ezekiel, 161, 168.
York, Joseph, 161, 168.
York, Samuel, 168.
York taken, 101.
Yorktown, 74.
    captured, 73.
Yarmon, John, 161.
Young, Daniel, 161.
Youngman, Jabez, 168.
Youngman, John, 168.

MAY 20 1941

www.ingramcontent.com/pod-product-compliance
Lightning Source LLC
Chambersburg PA
CBHW032227230426
43666CB00033B/1627